Cambridge English

Compact
Advanced

Student's Book without answers

Peter May

Charoenpong   Sansiri   (Siemon)

Cambridge University Press
www.cambridge.org/elt

Cambridge Assessment English
www.cambridgeenglish.org

Information on this title: www.cambridge.org/9781107418080

© Cambridge University Press and UCLES 2014

First published 2014

20 19 18 17 16 15 14 13 12

Printed in Malaysia by Vivar Printing

A catalogue record for this publication is available from the British Library

ISBN 978-1-107-41808-0 Student's Book without answers with CD-ROM
ISBN 978-1-107-41802-8 Student's Book with answers with CD-ROM
ISBN 978-1-107-41838-7 Teacher's Book with Teacher's Resources CD-ROM
ISBN 978-1-107-41828-8 Class Audio CDs (2)
ISBN 978-1-107-41782-3 Workbook without answers with Audio
ISBN 978-1-107-41790-8 Workbook with answers with Audio
ISBN 978-1-107-41819-6 Student's Book Pack (Student's Book with answers with CD-ROM and Class Audios (2))
ISBN 978-1-107-41831-8 Presentation Plus DVD-ROM
ISBN 978-1-107-41832-5 Interactive ebook: Student's Book with answers
ISBN 978-1-107-41794-6 Interactive ebook: Workbook with answers

Additional resources for this publication at www.cambridge.org/compactadvanced

Produced by Wild Apple

Front cover photographs by © Cultura Creative / Alamy (TR); © Amana images inc. / Alamy (CL);
© Andresr/Shutterstock (C); © PhotoAlto / Alamy (CR); © Stockbroker / Alamy (BR)

CONTENTS

MAP OF THE UNITS

	TOPICS	GRAMMAR	VOCABULARY
1	Events, issues & the media	Review of past, present & future tenses	Collocations Frequently confused words
2	Travel, customs & traditions	Participle clauses	Prefixes Academic expressions
3	Human behaviour & relationships	Review of reported speech	Collocations Idioms with *keep*
4	Money & business	Review of passive forms Causatives	Fixed phrases Phrasal verbs with *out* Money vocabulary
5	Health & sport	Conditionals including mixed forms & forms without *if*	Word building Suffixes Compound adjectives
6	The arts & entertainment	Review of verbs + *-ing* or infinitive	Collocations Frequently confused words
7	Nature & the environment	Inversion after negative adverbials	Collocations Phrasal verbs with *on* Idioms: nature
8	Education, learning & work	Relative clauses Introductory *it/what*	Affixes Spelling changes
9	Science & technology	Modals, including continuous & passive forms	Dependent prepositions Science lexis
10	Psychology & personality	Wishes & regrets	Three-part phrasal verbs Adjectives of personality

READING AND USE OF ENGLISH	WRITING	LISTENING	SPEAKING
Part 1: multiple-choice cloze Part 7: gapped text	Part 1 essay: get ideas, contrast links, checking	Part 4: multiple matching	Part 1: talking about past, present & future
Part 3: word formation Part 6: cross-text multiple matching	Part 2 report: planning, recommending	Part 2: sentence completion	Part 2: making comparisons
Part 4: key word transformations Part 5: multiple-choice questions	Part 2 letter: formal / informal / neutral style; layout	Part 1: short texts, multiple-choice questions	Part 3: suggesting, (dis)agreeing, asking for opinions
Part 2: open cloze Part 7: gapped text	Part 1 essay: addition links, achieving balance	Part 3: long text, multiple-choice questions	Part 4: expressing & justifying opinions
Part 3: word formation Part 8: multiple matching	Part 2 proposal: purpose links, text organisation	Part 2: sentence completion	Part 2: commenting on partner's pictures
Part 1: multiple-choice cloze Part 5: multiple-choice questions	Part 2 review: praising & criticising	Part 4: multiple matching	Part 1: expressing preferences, likes & dislikes
Part 4: key word transformations Part 7: gapped text	Part 1 essay: sentence adverbs paraphrasing notes	Part 1: short texts, multiple-choice questions	Part 3: giving examples, helping your partner
Part 3: word formation Part 8: multiple matching	Part 2 letter: formal language, text organisation	Part 2: sentence completion	Part 4: adding emphasis, hedging
Part 2: open cloze Part 5: multiple-choice questions	Part 2 report: result links, text organisation	Part 3: long text, multiple-choice questions	Part 2: speculating about present & past
Part 4: key word transformations Part 6: cross-text multiple matching	Part 1: concession, opening paragraphs	Part 4: multiple matching	Parts 3 & 4: negotiating, reaching a decision

INTRODUCTION

Who *Compact Advanced* is for

Compact Advanced is a short but highly intensive final preparation course for students planning to take the revised *Cambridge English: Advanced (CAE)* exam. It provides C1-level students with thorough preparation and practice of the grammar, vocabulary, language skills and exam skills needed. The course is particularly suitable for students of 16 and over.

What the Student's Book contains

Compact Advanced Student's Book has ten units for classroom study. Each unit covers practice for Reading and Use of English, Writing, Listening and Speaking. Interesting Reading and Listening texts cover topics that may appear in the *Cambridge English: Advanced (CAE)* exam, and are accompanied by activities that help develop the skills needed for understanding them and successfully completing the exam.

- **Writing** pages feature model answers and are built on a step-by-step approach to learning how to produce the different types of text needed in Writing Parts 1 and 2.
- **Speaking** activities are designed to improve fluency and accuracy, and to improve students' ability to express themselves with confidence and appropriacy.
- **Grammar** pages practise the structures that are needed for writing and speaking at this level, and also those frequently tested in Reading and Use of English Parts 1–4.
- **Vocabulary** input is at C1 level and is based on English Vocabulary Profile, while many grammar and vocabulary exercises are based on research from the Cambridge Learner Corpus (see below).
- *Quick steps* explain how to approach each exam task type, while *Exam tips* give useful advice on exam strategies.
- **Writing and Speaking guides** explain in detail what students can expect in these parts of the exam, and suggest how best to prepare and practise in each case. For Writing there are further sample tasks and model answers for each of the task types, while for Speaking there are lists of useful expressions for each part.
- The **Grammar reference** section gives clear explanations of grammar points students need to know for *Cambridge English: Advanced (CAE)*.
- A **wordlist** of 25–30 key words, informed by English Vocabulary Profile, is provided for each unit.
- The **CD-ROM** provides interactive exercises for extra language skills and practice.

Other course components

1. Two audio CDs contain listening material for the ten units of the Student's Book. Listening activities are indicated by an icon showing the CD and track numbers.
2. A *with-answers* edition which enables students to check their answers in the key at the back. For Listening tasks, the parts of the script that give the correct answers are underlined. Model answers to the Writing tasks are also included.
3. A **Teacher's Book**. This contains:
   - Step-by-step guidance for presenting and teaching all the material in the Student's Book. In some cases, alternative treatments and extension activities are suggested.
   - Complete answer keys for all activities in the ten units, with recording scripts for the listening material.
   - Five photocopiable progress tests: one for every two units in the Student's Book.
   - Sample tasks and model answers for all Writing questions.
4. A **Workbook** with audio to accompany the Student's Book. This contains:
   - Ten units for homework and self-study. Each unit has four pages of exercises, providing further practice and consolidation of the language and exam skills required for success in *Cambridge English: Advanced (CAE)*.
   - Exercises based on research from the Cambridge Learner Corpus.
   - Vocabulary input based on English Vocabulary Profile.
   - Sample tasks and model answers for all Writing questions.
   - In the *with-answers* edition, a full answer key and recording scripts with the answers underlined.
5. **Additional resources** for this publication can be found at www.cambridge.org/compactadvanced

The Cambridge Learner Corpus (CLC)

The Cambridge Learner Corpus (CLC) is a large collection of exam scripts written by students taking Cambridge English exams around the world. It forms part of the Cambridge International Corpus (CIC) and it has been built up by Cambridge University Press and Cambridge English Language Assessment.

Exercises and extracts from candidates' answers in *Compact Advanced* which are based on the CLC are indicated by this icon: ◉ .

Cambridge English: Advanced (CAE)

Reading and Use of English 1 hour 30 minutes

Parts 1 and 3 mainly test your vocabulary; Part 2 mainly tests grammar. Part 4 often tests both vocabulary and grammar. Parts 5–8 test reading comprehension.

Part	Task type	Questions	Format
1	Multiple-choice cloze	8	Fill each gap in a text from options A, B, C or D.
2	Open cloze	8	Fill each gap in a text with one word.
3	Word formation	8	Fill each gap in a text with the right form of a given word.
4	Key word transformation	6	Complete a sentence with a given word and up to five more words to mean the same as another sentence.
5	Multiple choice	6	Read a text followed by questions with four options: A, B, C or D.
6	Cross-text multiple matching	4	Read across four short texts and match prompts to the correct sections.
7	Gapped text	6	Read a text with six paragraphs removed. There are seven paragraphs to choose from.
8	Multiple matching	10	Read one or more texts. Match prompts to elements in the texts.

Writing 90 minutes

You have to do Part 1 plus one of the Part 2 tasks. In Part 2 you can choose one of questions 2–4.

Part	Task type	Words	Format
1	discursive essay	220–260	Write in response to two points given in an input text. Give reasons for your opinion
2	letter / email, proposal, report or review	220–260	Choose one from three tasks based on a given context and topic, with a clear purpose and target reader.

Listening about 40 minutes

You both hear and see the instructions for each task, and you hear all four parts twice.

Part	Task type	Questions	Format
1	Multiple choice	6	Three short extracts with two people talking for about a minute in three different situations. For each of two questions, you choose from answers A, B or C.
2	Sentence completion	8	One person speaking for about three minutes. Complete sentences by writing a word or short phrase.
3	Multiple choice	6	An interview or conversation of about four minutes. Choose from answers A, B, C or D.
4	Multiple matching	10	Five extracts of about 30 seconds each, with a common theme. For each extract there are two tasks. Choose from a list of eight possible answers.

Speaking 15 minutes

You do the Speaking test with one other candidate. There are two examiners, but one of them does not take part in the conversation.

Part	Task type	Minutes	Format
1	The examiner asks you questions.	2	Talk about yourself.
2	Talk on your own for one minute.	4	Talk about two pictures and then comment on the other candidate's pictures for about 30 seconds.
3	Talk to your partner.	4	A two-minute discussion. You then have a minute to make a decision.
4	Discuss topics connected with the theme of Part 3.	5	A discussion led by the examiner.

Breaking news
LISTENING

A Oil spill

B volcanic eruption

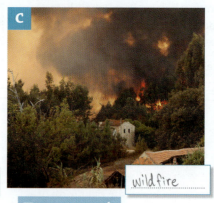

C wildfire

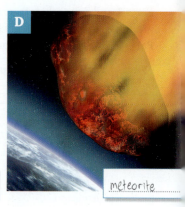

D meteorite

Part 4

1 Label the pictures *meteorite, oil spill, volcanic eruption* and *wildfire*. Then discuss the questions in pairs.

1 Which of these are natural events, and which – at least partly – are man-made?
2 How much media coverage does each receive? Why?
3 How would you feel if you witnessed each one? Use some of the C1-level adjectives in the box below.

> alarmed   appalled   disgusted   distressed   helpless
> hysterical   irritated   overwhelmed   speechless   unsafe

2 Look at the exam task instructions and options A–H in both tasks. Answer these questions.

1 How many speakers are there?
2 What information will you have to listen for in each task?
3 How many of the options in each task are <u>not</u> needed?

3 Note down words you might hear used about each of the options A–H in Task One, e.g. *an earthquake – ground, trembling*. Then highlight the key words (e.g. *number, injured*) in options A–H in Task Two and think of words associated with them, too.

4 🔘 **1.02** Listen and do the exam task. Listen particularly for the same ideas as those expressed by the words you highlighted in Exercise 3.

> **Quick steps to Listening Part 4**
> • Quickly read the instructions and the options in Tasks One and Two, identifying the key words in both.
> • Think of other words you might hear used to express those key words.
> • Listen for the answers to the questions in both tasks. Or, if you prefer, do one task on each listening.

Exam task

> You will hear five short extracts in which people are talking about unusual events they witnessed.

While you listen you must complete both tasks.

TASK ONE

For questions **1–5**, choose from the list (**A–H**) the event each speaker is talking about.

A an earthquake	
B an oil spill	Speaker 1 H 1 ✓
C a tropical storm	Speaker 2 E 2 Ⓓ
D a wildfire	Speaker 3 C 3 Ⓑ
E a volcanic eruption	Speaker 4 A 4 ✓
F a meteorite strike	Speaker 5 G 5 ✓
G a flood	
H a tornado	

TASK TWO

For questions **6–10**, choose from the list (**A–H**) what surprised each speaker most about the event.

A the number of people injured	
B the likely cause of the event	Speaker 1 Ⓕ D 6
C the sudden decrease in speed	Speaker 2 Ⓓ G 7
D the direction of travel	Speaker 3 Ⓐ B 8
E the extent of the damage	Speaker 4 Ⓑ F 9
F the relative lack of noise	Speaker 5 ✓ E 10
G the place where it happened	
H the number of unreported similar events	

> **Exam tip** ❯
>
> Don't choose an option just because you hear the same word or phrase. Listen for the same *idea*.

GRAMMAR

Review of verb tenses G *Page 88*

1 Explain the difference in meaning each time between sentences *a* and *b*. Name the different tenses used.

1 a I *see* my friends at the weekend. *Pre-sim*
   b I'*m seeing* my friends at the weekend. *Pre-con*
2 a The theme tune *began* when the programme *Past-sim* ended.
   b The theme tune *had begun* when the programme *Past-Per* ended.
3 a The press *were taking* photos when Melanie *Past-con* walked in.
   b The press *took* photos when Melanie walked in. *Past-sim*
4 a We'*ll be watching* that film when you get here. *future-con*
   b We'*ll watch* that film when you get here. *future-sim*
5 a Carla'*s written* a book about animals that can predict earthquakes. *Present per*
   b Carla'*s been writing* a book about animals that can predict earthquakes. *present per con*
6 a The thunderstorm *will have ended* by the time our plane takes off. *future-per*
   b The thunderstorm *will be ending* by the time our plane takes off. *future con*
7 a The economy *grew* rapidly when government policy changed. *Past-per sim*
   b The economy *had been growing* rapidly when government policy changed. *Past perfect con*
8 a When I'm 25, I'*ll work* abroad for several years. *future-sim*
   b When I'm 25, I'*ll have been working* abroad for *future-perfect-con* several years.

2 ◉ Correct the mistakes made by exam candidates. In some cases more than one answer is possible.

1 Do you come to the meeting next week? *Are coming*
2 I'm waiting for you at Vicenza Station tomorrow afternoon. *will be have known*
3 Barbara and I know each other for years. We went to primary school together.
4 In your memo you asked me to write a report, so now I'm going to send it to you. *I'm going*
5 I was waiting for 30 minutes when a man came and spoke to me. *had been*
6 I promise that when you'll come to visit me next summer, you'll have a wonderful holiday.
7 On Wednesday we went to St. Andrews, as I arranged to meet a friend of mine there. *had*
8 Club membership is falling so we are needing new members, especially young people. *need*

3 Choose the correct answer.

1 I *enjoy* / *enjoyed* / *have enjoyed* studying history since I was a child.
2 I'll look for a job when I *get* / *will get* / *will have got* my degree.
3 I'*m waiting* / *'ve been waiting* / *was waiting* in this queue for hours!
4 By the end of this century, we'*re exploring* / *'ll have explored* / *explore* distant planets.
5 My friend Stefan *was reading* / *has been reading* / *read* a book when I called at his house.
6 I'm not yet sure which subject I want to study, but I think I'*ll do* / *'m doing* / *'ll have done* maths.
7 When politicians at last realised what was happening, the climate *already became* / *had already become* / *had already been becoming* warmer.
8 By next July, I'*ll be living* / *'m living* / *'ll have been living* in this town for ten years.

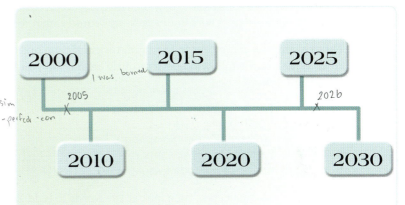

4 Mark some important past events in your life, e.g. starting secondary school, on the timeline above. Then tell your partner what you:

- were also doing and used to do at that time, e.g. *I was living in the city centre. I used to walk to school.*
- had done and had been doing before then.
- have done and have been doing since then.

5 Now put in some likely future events, e.g. *graduating, starting work*. Tell your partner what you:

- will also be doing then.
- will have done by then.
- will have been doing by then, and for how long.

Part 7

1 Look at these digital versions of printed reading material. Discuss these questions, giving reasons.

1 Which is more convenient: print or digital? Which is more enjoyable?

2 Which of the digital versions do you think are free? Which websites have a 'paywall', i.e. you have to pay for access?

3 Will any of the print versions have disappeared within ten years?

2 Quickly read the main text in the exam task and then options A–G. Which of the following have recently been rising, and which have been falling?

1 sales of news & current affairs magazines *D*
2 sales of printed books *F*
3 sales of European printed newspapers *E*
4 online advertising in newspapers *C*
5 worldwide sales of printed newspapers *G*

3 Read the third Quick step, then look at the words in bold after gaps 1, 2 & 3 and in options A, B & C. Answer these questions.

1 What kind of expressions are they?
2 How can each expression help you match the option to the gap?
3 Which similar expressions are used after gaps 4–6, and at the beginning of D–G?

4 Do the exam task, using the expressions in Exercise 3 to help you.

Quick steps to Reading and Use of English Part 7

- Look at the introduction to find out the text type and the topic.
- Quickly read the title, the main text and then options A–G, noting any topic links.
- For each gap, look for grammar links, e.g. reference words, linking expressions and matching verb tenses.
- Read the completed text to check it makes sense.

Exam task

You are going to read a newspaper article about online versions of printed publications. Six paragraphs have been removed from the article. Choose from the paragraphs **A–G** the one which fits each gap (**1–6**). There is one extra paragraph which you do not need to use.

The end of print may take some time

Peter Preston

Transition. It's a pleasant word and a calming concept. Change may frighten some and challenge others. But transition means going surely and sweetly from somewhere present to somewhere future. Unless, that is, it is newspapers' 'transition' to the online world, an uncertain and highly uncomfortable process – because, frankly, it may not be a process at all.

| 1 | E |

All of which may well be true, depending on timing, demography, geography and more. After all, everyone – from web academics to print analysts – says so. Yet pause for a while and count a few little things that don't quite fit.

| 2 | D |

As for news and current affairs magazines – which you'd expect to find in the eye of the digital storm – they had a 5.4% increase to report. In short, on both sides of the Atlantic, although some magazine areas went down, many showed rapid growth.

| 3 | F |

Yet, when booksellers examined the value of the physical books they sold over the last six months, they found it just 0.4% down. Screen or paper, then? It wasn't one or the other: it was both.

4	G

And even within Europe, different countries have different stories to tell. There's Britain, with a 10.8% drop in recent years (and a 19.6% fall for quality papers), but in Germany the decline has only been 7% all round – with a mere 0.8% lost to quality titles. And France shows only a 3.1% fall (0.8% at the quality end of the market).

5	C

Already 360 US papers – including most of the biggest and best – have built paywalls around their products. However, the best way of attracting a paying readership appears to be a deal that offers the print copy and digital access as some kind of joint package.

6	A

Of course this huge difference isn't good news for newspaper companies, as maintaining both an active website and an active print edition is difficult, complex and expensive. But newspaper brands still have much of their high profile in print; adrift on the web, the job of just being noticed becomes far harder.

Exam tip ⟩

Fill in the gaps you find easiest first to reduce the number you have to choose from.

A **In other words**, print is also a crucial tool in selling internet subscriptions. And its advertising rates raise between nine and ten times more money than online.

B Tales like **these** of young people abandoning newspaper-reading are wildly exaggerated. Turn to the latest National Readership Survey figures and you'll find nearly 5,000,000 people aged between 15 and 35 following the main national dailies.

C **Such** varying national trends may well reflect a situation far more complicated than the prophets of digital revolution assume. America's media analysts used to argue that booming online advertising revenues would pay for change and, along with lower production costs, make online newspapers a natural success. But now, with digital advertisements on newspaper sites actually dropping back, such assumptions seem like history.

D One is the magazine world, both in the UK and in the US. It ought to be collapsing, wrecked by the move to the tablets which fit existing magazine page sizes so perfectly. But, in fact, the rate of decline in magazine purchasing is relatively small, with subscriptions holding up strongly and advertising remarkably solid.

E But surely (you say) it is bound to happen eventually. Everybody knows that print newspaper sales are plummeting while visits to the same papers' websites keep on soaring. Just look at the latest print circulation figures. *The Daily Telegraph, The Guardian* and many of the rest are down overall between 8% and 10% year-on-year, but their websites go ever higher.

F You can discover a similar phenomenon when it comes to books. Kindle and similar e-readers are booming, with sales up massively this year. The apparent first step of transition couldn't be clearer.

G So if sales in that area have fallen so little, perhaps the crisis mostly affects newspapers? Yet again, though, the messages are oddly mixed. The latest survey of trends by the World Association of Newspapers shows that global circulation rose 1.1% last year (to 512 million copies a day). Sales in the West dropped back but Asia more than made up the difference.

Part 1

Collocations

1 In each of 1–6, which three verbs form collocations with the words on their right?

1	show / put / present / schedule	a TV programme
2	publish / submit / send in / contribute	a photo to a magazine
3	broadcast / perform / read / report	the news on TV
4	carry / print / feature / show	a newspaper story
5	draft / edit / broadcast / research	a magazine article
6	run / cover / promote / tell	a news story on TV

2 Complete the collocations in *italics* with the correct form of verbs from Exercise 1. In some cases more than one answer is possible.

1 The writer will have to ...edit... *the article* down to 1,000 words.
2 That's a lovely photo. Why don't you ...submit... it *to a nature magazine?*
3 Both channels ...broadcast... their main *news bulletin* live at ten o'clock.
4 The *documentary* was ...schedule... for 21.00, but will be shown at 21.30 instead.
5 It's best to ...draft... *an article*, make any changes, and then write a final version.
6 Channel 19 has decided not to ...run... *the story*. (cover / broadcast)
7 Our reporter Carla Montero has been ...cover... *this story* since the crisis began.
8 The web edition of the paper is ...running... *the story* on its front page. (reporting)

> **Quick steps to Reading and Use of English Part 1**
> • Look at the title and the example, then quickly read the text without filling in any gaps.
> • Look before and after each gap for words that collocate with the missing word.
> • Make sure your answers make sense.

3 Read quickly through the exam task. How does the text answer the question in the title?

4 Look at the example. Which word in the first sentence goes with *capture?* camera

5 Underline words that might go with missing words 1–8. Then do the exam task.

6 Discuss these questions.

1 If you witnessed a news event, would you photograph it? Would you submit the images to the media? Why/Why not?
2 How would you feel if the media published pictures from your Facebook page (for example) without permission?

Exam task

For questions **1–8**, read the text below and decide which answer (**A, B, C** or **D**) best fits each gap. There is an example at the beginning (**0**).

Example: **0**   **A** grasp   **B** capture   **C** seize   **D** trap

Should the media earn money from content they don't own?

Although digital cameras and camera phones have made it easier to (0) __B__ newsworthy events, it is social media that have revolutionised citizen photography. With news regularly breaking on social (1) _____ , some journalists are now turning to them as (2) _____ of images as fast-moving events occur.

Unfortunately, some reporters have published user-generated content (UGC) without permission. Despite official guidance that images (3) _____ on social media can be used without permission if there are exceptional circumstances or (4) _____ public interest, debate continues about whether this is ethical.

With research (5) _____ that around one in ten people would film or photograph a news event, it is clear that UGC has a major role to (6) _____ in the future of the media. However, if the media is to prevent its relationship with the public from souring, steps must be (7) _____ to ensure that people are properly rewarded for their work and that permission is always (8) _____ .

1	A	networks	B	complexes	C	frames	D	structures
2	A	bases	B	sources	C	roots	D	springs
3	A	deposited	B	planted	C	imposed	D	posted
4	A	sharp	B	strong	C	heavy	D	fierce
5	A	indicating	B	displaying	C	presenting	D	expressing
6	A	serve	B	apply	C	play	D	face
7	A	climbed	B	made	C	walked	D	taken
8	A	applied	B	sought (seek)	C	demanded	D	searched

> **Exam tip** ›
>
> Pencil in the words you choose on the question paper. This will make it easier to check the text makes sense when you finish.

1 SPEAKING

Frequently confused words

1 Choose the correct alternative in these exam candidates' sentences. Use your dictionary where necessary.

1 People are not *sensible / sensitive* enough to the problem of pollution.
2 He was *brought up / grown up* in Tunisia by a Sicilian mother.
3 This restaurant, as its name *infers / implies*, specialises in unusual dishes.
4 My income has *raised / risen* very little in the last four years.
5 I had to *assist / attend* an interview before the company offered me a job.
6 A bicycle is the most *economic / economical,* the cheapest and the easiest to park.
7 I *lied / lay* down on the couch and cried.
8 When I moved to my own apartment, I seized the *occasion / opportunity* to get rid of all those ugly objects.

Part 1 **S** *Page 107*

2 In pairs, decide whether these statements about Part 1 are True or False. Check your answers in the Speaking guide on page 107.

1 Part 1 usually lasts about two minutes.
2 There will be two examiners, but only one of them will ask you questions.
3 You have a conversation with the other candidate.
4 You must use formal language and call the examiner 'Madam' or 'Sir'.
5 You can learn your answers by heart and give a prepared speech.
6 You can invent information about yourself if it makes it easier for you to answer.

3 Look at these possible Part 1 questions. Which verb tenses would you mainly use to reply to each?

1 Where are you from?
2 What do you do here/there?
3 What do you think you'll be doing in five years' time?
4 How important do you think it is to speak more than one language?
5 What do you most enjoy about learning English?
6 Do you prefer to get the news from television, newspapers or the Internet?
7 What would you do if you suddenly became very rich?

4 🔊 **1.03** Listen to Cristina and Markus practising Part 1. Which of 1–5 below do you think describe each student's speaking? Write Yes (Y), No (N), or Possibly (P) in each box.

		Cristina	Markus
1	clear pronunciation, good use of stress and intonation	☐	☐
2	wide range of vocabulary, appropriate choice of words	☐	☐
3	links speech well, with little hesitation	☐	☐
4	generally correct grammar, wide range of structures	☐	☐
5	good communication skills	☐	☐

5 🔊 **1.04** Listen again and improve Markus's answers. Use your own ideas and some of these expressions:

- Well, as a matter of fact I …
- That's not an easy question to answer, but …
- I've never really thought about it before, but …
- Yes, I do/have actually. In fact, …
- No, I'm afraid I don't/haven't. But one day I'd like to …
- I haven't made my mind up yet, but I might …

> **Quick steps to Speaking Part 1**
> - Ask the examiner to repeat a question if necessary.
> - Reply with full answers, not just 'yes', 'no' or 'maybe'.
> - Use the right verb tense if asked about your past experiences or future plans.

6 Work in groups of three: one 'examiner' and two 'candidates'. The examiner asks each candidate questions from Exercise 3. Afterwards the examiner uses points 1–5 in Exercise 4 to comment on their performance, possibly suggesting improvements.

Exam tip ❯

Remember that one aim of Speaking Part 1 is to help you relax by getting you to talk about yourself.

Contrast links

1 Choose the two correct contrast links in italics in each sentence.

1 30 years ago almost everyone lived in the countryside *whereas* / *even though* / *while* nowadays most people live in cities.
2 *Whereas* / *Although* / *However* the poorest 10% have become poorer, the richest 1% are now even richer.
3 *In spite of* / *Despite the fact that* / *Even though* aid has increased, famine still exists.
4 A generation ago most doctors were male. *In contrast* / *While* / *However*, today the majority are female.
5 *Contrary to* / *Whereas* / *In spite of* what many people think, discrimination is still common.
6 By law all children must attend school. *Nevertheless* / *Despite this* / *Although*, many still work in the fields.
7 *In spite of the fact that* / *In contrast* / *Though* the war is over, the border region is still dangerous.
8 The south of the country is flooded. *Conversely* / *Contrary to* / *On the other hand*, the north is suffering from drought.

2 Complete the second sentence so that it means the same as the first sentence.

1 Many ordinary criminals have been released, though political prisoners remain in jail.
Whereas _many ordinary criminals have been released, political prisoners remain in jail._

2 Health care has improved, but it is still not up to international standards.
Even _though health care has improved, it is still not up to international standards._

3 Although unemployment has fallen, the number of homeless people has risen.
In spite _of the fact that unemployment has fallen, the number of homeless people has risen._

4 Though the workers' income is increasing, their quality of life is going down.
On the one hand _the worker's income is increasing, their quality of life is going down._

5 That country produces a lot of food, but ordinary people have little to eat.
Despite the fact _that country produces a lot of food, ordinary people have little to eat._

6 Some people say that we spend enough on overseas aid, but this isn't true.
Contrary _to what some people say, we don't spend enough on overseas._

7 In spite of the rise in fruit prices, farmers are getting paid less.
Although _the rise in fruit prices, farmer are getting paid less._

8 The Government bans all opposition but claims the country is a democracy.
The Government claims the country is a democracy. Conversely, _it bans all opposition._

3 What issue do the pictures illustrate? Write sentences using expressions from Exercise 1.

Part 1: essay *Page 99*

4 Look at the exam task instructions and the notes with it on page 15. Answer these questions.

1 What do you have to write about, and for whom?
2 Which aspects of the topic must you write about?
3 What can you include if you want to? What shouldn't you do with these?

Quick steps to writing a Part 1 essay

- Read all the instructions and the notes, underlining the key words.
- Think of as many relevant ideas as you can.
- Decide how many paragraphs you will need and put your ideas under headings, including those from the printed notes. Choose which of the three opinions to use.

Exam task

Write your answer in **220–260** words in an appropriate style.

You have listened to a discussion on how people in richer countries can be made more aware of poverty in other parts of the world. You have made the notes below:

> Ways of raising awareness of poverty as a global issue.
> - education
> - campaigns by charities
> - increased media coverage

> Some opinions expressed in the discussion:
>
> "Schools should teach every child the terrible effects of poverty."
>
> "We should support charities that expose the awful reality of poverty."
>
> "People would be shocked if they saw real poverty on TV every evening."

Write an essay for your tutor discussing **two** of the approaches in your notes. You should **explain which approach you think would be more effective, giving reasons** to support your opinion.

You may, if you wish, make use of the opinions expressed in the discussion, but you should use your own words as far as possible.

5 Read the model essay in the next column and answer these questions.

1 In which paragraph does the writer introduce the topic?
2 Which two of the notes does she use? In which paragraphs?
3 Which of the opinions expressed does she include, and where?
4 Which approach does she prefer? Where does she state this? What reasons does she give?
5 Is her essay the right length? Is it fairly formal or quite informal in style?
6 Which contrast links does she use?

Exam tip ›

Use a variety of contrast links to connect points in your essay.

There exists today an ever-widening wealth gap between different parts of the world, with an increasing number of people living in extreme poverty. Urgent measures are needed, and the first step must surely be to raise awareness in richer countries of just how desperate the situation is. To achieve this, there would appear to be two possible approaches.

Firstly, the media could cover world poverty much more frequently and in far greater depth. Currently, television rarely focuses on this human tragedy, despite the awful conditions in which hundreds of millions of people spend their entire lives. Regular in-depth reports, however, would surely bring it home to viewers that this appalling situation never goes away, leading to greater pressure on governments to take steps such as increasing overseas aid.

Schools could also have an important role to play. Although it is essential that pupils are taught about the social problems of their own country, attention should also be paid to the difficulties of those, especially children, in poorer nations. Students need to learn why such terrible living conditions exist, both by studying the history of those countries and by looking at the political, economic and social factors that make poverty so difficult to eliminate.

Nevertheless, relying on the education system would take many years to bring results, whereas change is needed right now. It should also involve the whole population, not just young people. Only the media can have this immediate impact, and nowadays it is only the media that almost everyone pays attention to.

6 You are going to write your own essay. To help you get ideas, discuss these questions and make notes.

1 Which are the worst examples of poverty that you know about?
2 Which had most impact on you: reading or hearing about them, or seeing images?
3 Which do you think influence people's feelings about global issues most: schools and universities, charities, or the media? Why?

7 Look at the third Quick step and plan your essay. Here is one possible paragraph plan:

1 Introduction: the topic
2 Charities: direct experience, tell the truth, opinion 1
3 Education: scarce resources, contrast rich/poor, opinion 2
4 Conclusion: charities more effective + reasons

8 Write your **essay** in **220–260** words in an appropriate style. When you have finished, check it for the following:

- correct length
- coverage of all the necessary points
- good organisation into well-linked paragraphs
- a wide range of structures and vocabulary
- correct grammar, spelling and punctuation
- appropriate style of language
- positive effect on the reader.

2 Travels and traditions
READING AND USE OF ENGLISH

Part 6

1 Put these reasons for travelling to distant places in order, from least to most important.

- beautiful countryside
- friendly people
- impressive architecture
- inexpensive
- interesting wildlife
- learning the language
- local culture
- pleasant climate
- doing voluntary work

2 Discuss these questions about the photos, which show international volunteers working in developing countries.

1 What kind of people do you think the volunteers are?
2 Why do you think they have chosen to do this work?
3 In what ways might their work help the local people?
4 How will the experience benefit the volunteers?
5 Would you like to do this kind of work during a 'gap year'? Why / Why not?

> **Quick steps to Reading and Use of English Part 6**
> - Read all four texts for gist and main ideas.
> - Underline the key words in the items.
> - Remember there may be evidence for an answer in more than one part of the extract.

3 Look at the exam task and answer these questions.

1 Are the texts written by the same person?
2 What is the link between them?
3 What style are they written in?
4 What do the questions focus on?
5 What do you have to compare and contrast?

4 Quickly read the four texts. Which of the points you discussed in Exercise 2 do they mention? How far do you agree with what they say?

5 The texts contain expressions often used in academic writing. Find words with the following meanings.

1 although (A)
2 small and unimportant (A)
3 for this reason (A)
4 mention without talking about directly (A)
5 caused to behave in a particular way (A)
6 in a morally correct way (A)
7 improved (B)
8 description of a situation (B)
9 a sign of something (bad) (D)
10 written or spoken communication (D)

6 Underline the key words in questions 1–4, e.g. *similar, A, impact, local people*. Then do the exam task.

> **Exam tip ›**
>
> You can use the same option for more than one answer.

Exam task

You are going to read four texts about international volunteers. For questions **1–4**, choose from the writers A–D. The writers may be chosen more than once.

Which writer	
takes a similar view to writer A on the likely impact of voluntary work on local people's lives?	**1** D
expresses a different view from the others on why people do international voluntary work?	**2** D
has the same opinion as writer A about the possible long-term effects on the volunteers?	**3** C
shares writer C's concern about who the volunteers tend to be?	**4** B

Volunteer tourism

Four academic writers discuss the topic of international voluntary work.

A

It is hard to argue that the actual contribution to development amounts to a great deal directly. Whilst volunteer tourists can get involved in building homes or schools, they have usually paid a significant fee for the opportunity to be involved in this work: money that, if donated to a local community directly, could potentially pay for a greater amount of labour than the individual volunteer could ever hope to provide. This is especially so in the case of gap years, in which the level of technical skill or professional experience required of volunteers is negligible. Hence, it is unsurprising that many academic studies allude to the moral issue of whether gap year volunteering is principally motivated by altruism – a desire to benefit the society visited – or whether young people aim to generate 'cultural capital' which benefits them in their careers. However, the projects may play a role in developing people who will, in the course of their careers and lives, act ethically in favour of those less well-off.

B

Volunteering may lead to greater international understanding; enhanced ability to solve conflicts; widespread and democratic participation in global affairs through global civic society organisations; and growth of international social networks among ordinary people. In this scenario, the whole is greater than the sum of its parts, an outcome where benefits accrue to volunteers and host communities, and contribute to the global greater good. However, if volunteering is largely limited to individuals of means from wealthier areas of the world, it may give these privileged volunteers an international perspective, and a career boost, but it will do little for people and communities who currently lack access to international voluntary work. Those who volunteer will continue to reap its benefits, using host organisations and host communities as a rung on the ladder of personal advancement.

C

At its worst, international volunteering can be imperialist, paternalistic charity, volunteer tourism, or a self-serving quest for career and personal development on the part of well-off Westerners. Or it can be straightforward provision of technical assistance for international development. At its best, international volunteering brings benefits (and costs) to individual volunteers and the organisations within which they work, at the same time as providing the space for an exchange of technical skills, knowledge, and cross-cultural experience in developing communities. Most significantly, volunteering can raise awareness of, and a lifelong commitment to combating, existing unequal power relations and deep-seated causes of poverty, injustice, and unsustainable development.

D

Volunteer tourism seems to fit well with the growth of life strategies to help others. Such limited strategies, aimed at a humble 'making a difference', can appear positive and attractive in an anti-political climate. The personal element appears positive – it bypasses big government and eschews big business. Yet it also bypasses the democratic imperative of representative government and reduces development to individual acts of charity, most often ones that seek to work around rather than transform the situations of poor, rural societies. Cynicism at the act of volunteering is certainly misplaced. The act of volunteer tourism may involve only simple, commendable charity. However, where volunteer tourism is talked up as sustainable development and the marketing of the gap-year companies merges into development thinking, this is symptomatic of a degradation of the discourse of development. The politics of volunteer tourism represents a retreat from a social understanding of global inequalities and the poverty lived by so many in the developing word.

GRAMMAR

Participle clauses *Page 89*

1 Match the underlined participle clauses with purposes a–h. Then rewrite the sentences using the words in brackets.

1 <u>Feeling tired</u>, we eventually stopped for a rest.
2 A lion approached, <u>looking hungry</u>.
3 <u>Not wanting to take any chances</u>, they kept away from the cliff edge.
4 <u>Noticing the huge hole in the road</u>, Carlos hit the brakes.
5 <u>Having bought our tickets</u>, we boarded the ferry.
6 <u>Handled carefully</u>, those creatures are not dangerous.
7 The bridge collapsed, <u>leaving us stranded on the island.</u>
8 <u>Located in Chile and Peru</u>, the Atacama is the world's driest desert.

a to state a condition (*as long as*)
b to give a negative reason (*in order*)
c to express a result (*so*)
d to say what we had done before we did something else (*and then*)
e to replace a relative clause (*which*)
f to emphasise that one thing happened just after another (*as soon as*)
g to give a reason (*because*)
h to reduce two sentences to one (*it*)

2 Find the mistakes in these sentences containing participle clauses and correct them.

1 Driven crazy by thirst, we read how the crew survive in an open boat.
2 Barking loudly, Sean was approached by a large dog.
3 After being washed in hot water, I noticed my clothes had turned pink.
4 Scared of heights, tall buildings are places that Joey avoids.
5 Having finished my breakfast, Tanya and I set off on foot.
6 Not wishing to damage the plants, the footpath is used by walkers.
7 Watered every day, you will find these plants grow quickly.
8 Running to catch the train, my ticket fell onto the platform.

3 Join the sentences using participle clauses.

1 Marta looked tired. She said she had been travelling all night.
2 We were climbing in the mountains. We saw an eagle fly past.
3 You can wear this jacket with matching trousers. It looks great.
4 Joaquin is tall. He could see over the crowd's heads.
5 I was exhausted by the journey. I slept for 18 hours.
6 Our vehicle broke down. That left us stuck in the forest.
7 My sister has studied Mandarin for five years. She speaks it well.
8 Jack didn't have anyone to talk to. He felt lonely.

4 Use participle clauses to rewrite the underlined parts of the text.

(1) <u>We left at 6 am and</u> we headed north. (2) <u>We didn't want to waste time, so</u> we walked up the steep valley (3) <u>which led to the foothills of the Central Range.</u> (4) <u>Once we'd reached</u> the top of those, we saw the much higher peaks ahead. (5) <u>They were covered in snow and</u> looked forbidding. (6) <u>We descended to a river where</u> we crossed a narrow stone bridge, (7) <u>which was built centuries ago</u>, then began climbing again. After another hour, (8) <u>because we were feeling hungry</u>, we stopped for a snack. Suddenly we noticed dark clouds gathering over the peaks. (9) <u>As we realised that would mean more snow</u>, we discussed our next move. (10) <u>After we'd decided to carry on</u>, we continued our trek uphill. (11) <u>When I look back at that moment</u>, I sometimes wonder whether that was the right decision (12) <u>if one bears in mind</u> what followed. But climbing is about taking risks, and we all survived to tell the tale.

5 Write a short account of an eventful journey. Include as many participle clauses as you can, e.g. *Setting off from … Having missed…, Realising …, Not wanting to … .*

2 READING AND USE OF ENGLISH

Prefixes

1 👁 Correct the mistakes made by exam candidates.

1 The host families are located unconveniently far away from the school.
2 The local chief of police says that the number of arrests has disincreased.
3 We have to insure that the jobs provided are suitable for our students.
4 Some of the information in the article is unprecise.
5 Do not think of yourself as uncapable of driving a car.
6 Closing the canteen early would unevitably leave many students feeling hungry.
7 The promised 'lively social programme' during our stay was inexistent.
8 The notion of a pop star having a private life would seem as irrealistic as a fairy tale.

2 Add the correct prefixes from the box to form C1-level words. You do not need to use all of them.

| anti | bi | dis | inter | il | mis | mono | out |
| over | post | re | under | | | | |

1 The hotel staff are ...paid and deserve an immediate rise.
2 The old industrial area will be ...developed as a shopping mall.
3 It's a lovely beach but it's ...crowded in summer.
4 The advertisement ...led us into thinking the flights were free.
5 Shanghai has ...lingual street signs, in Mandarin and English.
6 On the coast, foreign tourists ...number local people.
7 Downtown at night, there's a lot of ...social behaviour such as people shouting.
8 In other cultures, people ...act with each other differently.

3 Work in small groups. Match the correct prefixes in Exercise 2 with these meanings, then form as many words as you can with each prefix.

a) again   b) against   c) between
d) more / bigger / better   e) not enough
f) too much   g) two   h) wrongly

Part 3

Quick steps to Reading and Use of English Part 3
• Quickly read the title, the example and the rest of the text.
• Decide on the part of speech and if it is positive or negative.
• Try adding different prefixes and/or suffixes to the word in capitals, or forming compounds.

4 Look at the exam task instructions and quickly read the text. Why did the writer go to Norway?

5 Answer these questions about the example (0), then do the exam task.

1 What part of speech is needed and how is it formed?
2 Does the sentence indicate a positive or a negative meaning?
3 What prefix, therefore, is needed?

Exam task

For questions **1–8**, read the text below. Use the word given in capitals at the end of some of the lines to form a word that fits in the gap **in the same line**. There is an example at the beginning **(0)**.

Write your answers **IN CAPITAL LETTERS**.

Example: 0 UNSPOILT

Norway's Alps

We sailed along the beautiful **(0)** ⸺ coast of northern Norway until we reached the town of Tromso, over 300 kilometres inside the Arctic Circle. With its brightly-coloured wooden houses set against a **(1)** ⸺ of snow-capped mountains, it was a remarkable sight. — **SPOIL** / **GROUND**

In the afternoon, we travelled to the Lyngen Alps where the **(2)** ⸺ scenery took my breath away. Given the remote location, our accommodation there was surprisingly **(3)** ⸺ and the large meal of fresh fish we were served that evening was of an **(4)** ⸺ high standard for such a small hotel. The next day, refreshed after a wonderful **(5)** ⸺ sleep of nearly nine hours, I headed for the practice slope, where **(6)** ⸺ cross-country skiers like myself had to learn how to climb uphill with skis on. That far north towards the end of May, there was **(7)** ⸺ daylight – and it was my **(8)** ⸺ to go midnight skiing. — **COMPARE** / **LUXURY** / **EXPECT** / **BREAK** / **EXPERIENCE** / **INTERRUPT** / **INTEND**

Exam tip ›

Read through the completed text to check it all makes sense and is grammatically correct.

2 LISTENING

Part 2

1 Look at the pictures of the annual Inti Raymi (Festival of the Sun) in the Peruvian city of Cuzco, high in the Andes mountains. Answer the questions below using some of the words in the box.

> applause celebrations ceremony
> costumes gathering feast itinerary
> onlookers parade participants
> procession rehearsal speeches
> tradition volunteers

1 What can you see in each picture and what is happening?
2 Why do you think this is an important event to the local people?
3 How do you think they are feeling, and why?

Quick steps to Listening Part 2
- Read the introduction, the title and the question to get an idea of the context.
- The first time you listen, pencil in your answers on the question paper.
- The second time you listen, check your answers and make necessary changes.

2 Study the exam task. For each question:
- underline the key words
- decide what kind of word, e.g plural noun, is needed.

3 🔘 **1.05** Do the exam task. Listen for expressions similar to the key words you underlined, but write no more than three words for each answer.

Exam task

You will hear a research student called Ava O'Neill talking about visiting Cuzco in Peru. For questions **1–8**, complete the sentences with a word or short phrase.

The ancient city of Cuzco

The words **(1)** .... are sometimes used to describe the city because of its historic buildings.

Cuzco was originally designed in the shape of **(2)** ....

The Incas built houses in Cuzco without **(3)** .... to keep out the cold.

Ava says the **(4)** .... in Cuzco was a problem for some people but not for her.

Watching the rehearsals, Ava found the **(5)** .... particularly impressive.

Ava was surprised by the wide range of **(6)** .... when the main parade began.

Ava believes the builders of the walls first made **(7)** .... of certain stones.

Ava had read there were no **(8)** .... at the ancient Festival of the Sun.

Exam tip ›

Write the words you hear; don't try to rephrase them.

4 Think of a festival that you have been to, or one that you know about. Tell your partner where and when it happens, what it consists of, and why people enjoy it.

2 SPEAKING

Making comparisons

1 Rewrite these sentences about customs and traditions so that the second sentence means the same as the first.

1 The British drink just as much tea as they did in the past.

The British don't drink ....

....

2 They carry umbrellas because rain is a lot more frequent there.

They carry umbrellas because it rains

....

3 The USA has slightly fewer public holidays than some other countries.

The USA doesn't have ....

....

4 Having a lot of brothers and sisters isn't nearly as common as it used to be.

Having a lot of brothers and sisters is

....

5 Years ago, people were far more likely to marry young than they are today.

Today, people are not ....

....

6 Diwali is a great deal more widely celebrated internationally than it was.

20 years ago, Diwali was nowhere

....

7 Some think April Fool's Day is twice as much fun as St Valentine's Day.

Some think St Valentine's Day ....

....

2 Tell your partner about customs and traditions in your country. Use comparative forms from Exercise 1 to describe changes and make comparisons with other countries.

Part 2 **S** *Page 108*

> ### Quick steps to Speaking Part 2
> - Listen to the instructions and choose two of the photos to discuss.
> - If you don't know a word paraphrase it, e.g. *The blue object next to …*
> - Do all the task: compare the photos **and** answer the questions.

3 🔊 **1.06** Read the exam task instructions. Then listen to Luisa and Emilia talking about two of the pictures and answer these questions.

1 Which photos does Luisa decide to compare?
2 Does she do both parts of the task?
3 How does Emilia answer her question?

4 🔊 **1.06** Listen again. Which of the comparative structures in Exercise 1 do Luisa and Emilia use?

5 Work in pairs and do the exam task using pictures 1 and 3. Then change roles and do the task using pictures 2 and 3.

Exam task

Each of you will be given three pictures. You have to talk about **two** of them on your own for about a minute, and also to answer a question briefly about your partner's pictures.

Candidate A, it's your turn first. Here are your pictures. They show people with presents in different situations. Compare two of the pictures, and say what significance the presents might have for the people, and how they might be feeling.

Candidate B, who do you think has given the most thought to their choice of present?

> What significance might the presents have for these people? How might they be feeling?

Exam tip ❯

Remember that the questions the examiner asks you are also written above the photos.

2 WRITING

Part 2: report *Page 103*

1 Complete the <u>underlined</u> expressions with the words in the box.

> aims balance consider course outlines purpose recommend
> recommendation recommending short solution sum

1 <u>To .... up</u>, immediate action is required.
2 <u>My .... is that</u> visitors should always book ahead.
3 <u>One possible .... would be to</u> impose strict parking regulations.
4 <u>The .... of this</u> report is to assess the town's sports facilities.
5 <u>On .... ,</u> our overall reaction to the proposals is positive.
6 <u>This report ....</u> the range of job opportunities available.
7 <u>I strongly .... that</u> further research be carried out.
8 <u>In ....</u> we thoroughly enjoyed our stay at the resort.
9 The organisers <u>should .... </u> improving facilities for the disabled.
10 <u>The best .... of action would be to</u> lower the admission fees.
11 <u>This report .... to</u> provide an overview of the current situation.
12 <u>I have no hesitation in .... </u> this superb historic site to travellers.

2 Put the underlined expressions from Exercise 1 into the correct columns (more than one answer might be possible). Which of these expressions are quite formal?

Introduction	Recommendations and suggestions	Conclusion
....	....	....
....	....	....
....	....	....
....	....	....
....	....	....

3 What situations are shown in these pictures? For each one, write a recommendation and a suggestion using expressions from the table above.

4 Answer these questions about the exam task.

1 What must you write about?
2 Who are you writing for and why do they want a report?
3 What points must you include?

Exam task

> In your English class, you have been discussing festivals around the world. Your tutor has asked you to write a report on a popular festival in your country that may interest other students. Your report should:
>
> - describe the event, saying where and when it takes place
> - say how popular it is and why
> - outline some changes you think should be made.
>
> Write your **report** in **220–260** words in an appropriate style.

5 Quickly read the model report opposite and match headings A–D below with with paragraphs 1–4. Then answer the questions.

> A Finding out about chocolate
> B Recommendations
> C Introduction
> D The artistic applications of chocolate

1 Does the writer have a generally positive attitude to the festival?
2 Is it written in an appropriate style?

A sweet festival in Germany

1 ....

The aim of this report is to provide information on the ChocolArt festival, held each December in the picturesque university town of Tübingen in south-west Germany.

2 ....

As the name implies, this festival is about chocolate as art, with the world's greatest chocolate makers all competing to produce the most impressive creations. There are also fascinating exhibitions of chocolate sculptures, examples of products from around the world and, in the evenings, projections on the walls of the town centre buildings. Shop windows display chocolate fountains, and there is even a chocolate theatre.

3 ....

Attracting over 200,000 visitors annually, the festival has something to appeal to all age groups. For adults there are chocolate-making lessons, while children can visits chocolate workshops and sample such delights as edible smartphones. There are also opportunities to learn about the people who produce the ingredients of chocolate, and how the policy of Fairtrade can make a real difference to their lives. This is often of particular interest to local students.

4 ....

In conclusion, this is an informative and hugely enjoyable festival that leaves a pleasant taste in the mouth. I noticed, however, that rather fewer stalls gave free samples than in previous years and consequently, I would recommend the organisers encourage stallholders to be a little more generous in future. I would also suggest they consider changing the dates from chilly December to a warmer month – even if some of that delicious chocolate might melt.

6 Read the model report again and answer these questions.

1 What expressions does the writer use to
   a) state the purpose of the report?
   b) make comparisons?
   c) conclude the report?
   d) make a recommendation and a suggestion?
2 Find one participle clause in the first paragraph and another in the third paragraph.
3 Which expressions indicate the writer's attitude to the festival?

7 Look at these exam task instructions and answer the questions in Exercise 4 about it.

Exam task

You work for an agency that promotes your country's tourist industry abroad. Your manager has asked you to write a report on an interesting, lesser-known sight in your country. Your report should describe the place or building, explain its significance to your country, and suggest ways it could become better-known internationally.

Write your **report** in **220–260** words in an appropriate style.

Quick steps to writing a Part 2 report
- Note down any facts you know about the topic, plus any personal experiences you could mention.
- Decide how many paragraphs you need, and whether to use headings.
- In the first paragraph, state the purpose of your report.
- Present your ideas in a logical sequence and in a fairly formal style.
- End with a suitable conclusion, making recommendations and/or suggestions.

8 Discuss these questions in small groups.

1 Which are the most interesting lesser-known sights in your country?
2 What facts do you know about them?
3 If you have visited them, what are your most vivid memories?
4 How could those places attract more visitors from abroad?

9 Choose one of the sights you discussed in Exercise 8. Then look at the Quick steps and plan your report.

Exam tip ▸

Think of a good title that will indicate to readers the content of your report and encourage them to read it.

10 Write your report. When you have finished, check your work as in Unit 1, Writing Exercise 8 on page 15.

Collocations

1 Read sentences 1–6 below. Which adjectives in italics do not collocate with the nouns? Which group should the adjective be in?

1 Olivia is a *close / school / true / childhoood /(brief)/ fair-weather* **friend**.
2 Liam is my *new /(family)/ marriage / previous / dancing / former* **partner**.
3 Nowadays there are far more *lone / adoptive /(personal) / single / foster / step-* **parents**.
4 I grew up in a typical *two-parent / close-knit / extended / nuclear /(absent)/ dysfunctional* **family**.
5 Lola is Miguel's only *immediate / distant / blood / close /(strong)/ living* **relative**.
6 I think Chandra and Ajay will have a *stable / lifelong /(mutual)/ stormy / long-term / close* **relationship**.

2 Compare two of the pictures and say what kind of relationship the people have. Then listen while your partner does the same with the other two pictures.

Part 1

3 Look at the exam task. Study the introduction to each extract and the first line of each question, then answer these questions.

1 What is the situation in each extract?
2 Who will you hear?
3 What will they be talking about?
4 What is the focus of each question? e.g. 1 *a reason*, 2 *giving advice*

4 ▶ **1.07** Listen and do the exam task.

Exam task

You will hear three different extracts. For questions **1–6**, choose the answer (**A**, **B** or **C**) which fits best according to what you hear. There are two questions for each extract.

Extract One

You hear a couple, Jack and Emily, discussing a problem he has at work.

1 Why did Jack and a colleague fall out?
   A The man had complained to the boss about Jack.
   B The firm had selected Jack for a particular task.
   C Jack had forced the man to resign from his post.

2 Emily advises Jack to
   A talk calmly to the man about the issue.
   B let her speak to the man at lunchtime.
   C avoid seeing the man if at all possible.

Extract Two

You hear two people discussing a news story they have just watched on TV.

3 What was the news story mainly about?
   A how to tell when people are lying
   B circumstances in which people tend to lie
   C the types of people who are most likely to lie

4 What surprises the woman about the information in the story?
   A the high number of lies people tell
   B how inventive some criminals can be
   C a technique the police use to detect lies

Extract Three

You hear two students, Amelia and Ollie, in a café talking about flat sharing.

5 They both think that finding the right flatmates
   A is inevitably a slow process.
   B means you will become close friends.
   C can create a wider social circle.

6 What is Amelia's attitude to standards of tidiness and cleanliness?
   A Everyone should adopt those of the tidiest person.
   B It can be annoying when people criticise those of others.
   C Men tend to be less concerned about them than women.

3 GRAMMAR

Reported speech Page 90

1 Read these sentences reporting a further conversation between Amelia and Ollie from the Listening task. Rewrite them in direct speech, underlining the words that change.

Example: Amelia said she'd found her
flatmates on that website.

"*I found my flatmates on this website.*"

1 She asked Ollie whether he was still living in the same flat.
2 He said that he wasn't. He'd moved out the previous week.
3 She wanted to know why he'd left.
4 He explained that he hadn't been able to study properly.
5 She asked what the problem had been.
6 He replied that a few months earlier his flatmate had started learning the violin.
7 She enquired whether he'd found a quieter place by then.
8 He said he had, and that he thought he'd enjoy living there.

2 🔵 **1.08** Listen and check your answers. How do they differ from the reported speech versions?

Example: she → I   had found → found
her → my   that → this

3 👁 Correct the mistakes in these sentences written by exam candidates. In some cases more than one answer is possible. Two sentences are correct.

1 Some students **suggested** ~~to go~~ *going* sightseeing on Monday.
2 Your brochure **said** that I ~~got~~ a room in a high-class hotel.
3 I arrived late and my boss **warned** *would get* me not to do that again. ✓
4 She **asked** me whether she could look after the kids from time to ✓ time.
5 He **threatened** ~~his daughter~~ *his daughter* not to speak to ~~her~~ again if she married that man.
6 The radio **told** us ~~to not~~ *not to* go anywhere because of the snow.
7 The electric company **apologised** for not ~~have~~ *having* told me the lights would go out.
8 Socrates never **promised** that his students ~~will~~ *would* actually learn anything specific.

4 Rewrite the sentences using the reporting verbs in bold in Exercise 3. Begin 'He …' or 'She …'. More than one answer is possible.

1 'I didn't break your coffee mug.'
2 'Can I help you?'
3 'Let's share this flat together.'
4 'I'm sorry I woke you up.'
5 'I'll pay you back at the end of this month.'
6 'You shouldn't touch this wire while the electricity is on.'
7 'If you don't get out now, I'll call the police.'
8 'Tomorrrow's Saturday. Don't wake me before noon.'

5 Complete these sentences about yourself using the reporting verbs in italics. Then write what was actually said. Compare answers with a partner.

Example: I was late so I explained … that I'd missed the bus.
'I'm afraid I missed the bus.'

1 I was tired so I *refused* ....
2 My best friend *invited* ....
3 My sister/cousin *complained* ....
4 My mother *reminded* ....
5 The doctor *advised* ....
6 A friend of mine *admitted* ....
7 One of my relatives who had a car *offered* ....
8 A friend who had a new phone *recommended* ....

3 READING AND USE OF ENGLISH

Part 5

1 In each of these situations, how often do you

   a) talk to people?   b) use a device such as a mobile phone?

Quick steps to Reading and Use of English Part 5
- Read the text for gist only.
- Read each question or unfinished statement, but not options A–D.
- Read the relevant part of the text. Answer in your own words.
- Choose the option closest to your own answer.

---

2 Look at the exam task instructions and then quickly read the text. What is the writer's answer to the question in the title?

3 Look at this example item (remember, there is no example in the exam) and answer these questions. Then do the exam task.

  1 Which is the relevant part of the text?
  2 Why is answer C correct?
  3 Why is each of A, B and D incorrect?

    What was the writer's reaction to the scene he describes in the first paragraph?
  A He was concerned that it mainly involved young people.   ✗
  B He wondered whether the same things happened in real life.   ✗
  C He thought those who were walking looked uncomfortable.   ✓
  D He was pleased to be in a place where there was no noise.   ✗

Exam tip ›

Look for evidence that your answer is right, and also that the other options are wrong.

Exam task

You are going to read a newspaper article. For questions 1–6, choose the answer (**A, B, C** or **D**) which you think fits best according to the text.

Now everyone is connected, is this the death of conversation?

As our meeting places fall silent, save for tapping on screens, it seems we have mistaken connection for the real thing

Simon Jenkins

I first noticed it in a restaurant. The place was oddly quiet, and at one table a group sat with their heads bowed, their eyes hooded and their hands in their laps. I then realised that every one, whatever their age group, was gazing at a handheld phone or tablet. People strolled in the street outside likewise, with arms at right angles, necks bent and heads in awkward postures. Mothers with babies were doing it. Students in groups were doing it. The scene resembled something from an old science-fiction film. There was no conversation.

Every visit to California convinces me that the digital revolution is over, by which I mean it is won. Everyone is connected. *The New York Times* last week declared the death of conversation. While mobile phones may at last be falling victim to considerate behaviour, this is largely because even talk is considered too intimate a contact. No such bar applies to emailing, texting, messaging, posting and tweeting. It is ubiquitous, the ultimate connectivity, the brain wired full-time to infinity.

The MIT professor and psychologist Sherry Turkle claims that her students are close to mastering the art of maintaining eye contact with a person while texting someone else. It is like an organist playing different tunes with hands and feet. To Turkle, these people are 'alone together … a tribe of one'. Anyone with 3,000 Facebook friends has none.

The audience in many theatres now sit, row on row, with lit machines in their laps, looking to the stage occasionally but mostly scrolling and tapping away. The same happens at meetings and lectures, in coffee bars and on jogging tracks. Psychologists have identified this as 'fear of conversation', and have come up with the term 'conversational avoidance devices' for headphones.

In consequence, there is now a booming demand for online 'conversation' with robots and artificial voices. Mobiles come loaded with customised 'boyfriends' or 'girlfriends'. People sign up with computerised dating advisors, even claim to fall in love with their on-board GPS guides. A robot seal *line 46* can be picked up in online stores to sit and listen to elderly individuals talk, tilting its head and blinking in sympathy.

In his *Conversation: A History of a Declining Art*, Stephen Miller notes that public discourse is now dominated by ill-tempered disagreement, by 'intersecting monologues'. Anger and lack of restraint are treated as assets in public debate, in place of a willingness to listen and adjust one's point of view. Politics thus becomes a platform of rival angers. American politicians are ever more polarised, reduced to conveying a genuine hatred for each other.

All that said, the death of conversation has been announced as often as that of the book. As far *line 61* back as the 18th century, the literary figure Samuel Johnson worried that the decline of political conversation would lead to violent civil disorder. Writing 70 years ago, George Orwell concluded that 'the trend of the age was away from creative communal amusements and toward solitary mechanical ones'. Somehow we have muddled through.

The 'post-digital' phenomenon, the craving for live experience, is showing a remarkable vigour. The US is a place of ever greater congregation and migration, to parks, beaches and restaurants, to concerts, rock festivals, ball games. Common interest groups, springing up across the country, desperately seek escape from the digital dictatorship, using Facebook and Twitter not as destinations but as route maps to meet up with real people.

Somewhere in this cultural mix I am convinced the desire for friendship will preserve the qualities essential for a civilised life, qualities of politeness, listening and courtesy. Those obsessed with fashionable connectivity and personal avoidance are not escaping reality. They may be unaware of it but deep down they, too, still want someone to talk to.

1 The writer believes the main reason for the decreasing use of mobile phones is
   A the realisation that it is bad manners to use them in public places.
   B an overall reduction in the use of electronic devices for communication.
   C the fact that people are increasingly reluctant to speak to one another.
   D a general feeling that they are rapidly becoming obsolete technology.

2 According to Sherry Turkle, certain people nowadays are
   A determined to return to a more traditional form of social structure.
   B electronically connected but isolated from genuine human interaction.
   C incapable of forming true friendships except through social media.
   D more skillful at communicating with others via music than in words.

3 The writer uses the example of the 'seal' in line 46 to show
   A how far the technology of artificial intelligence has progressed.
   B that electronic companions are regarded as non-threatening.
   C how robots can help those unable to find a romantic partner.
   D the negative impact of internet search engines on conversation.

4 What point is made in the sixth paragraph about the current nature of public discussion?
   A Speakers are expected to behave aggressively towards each other.
   B Political parties are becoming increasingly extreme in their views.
   C The behaviour of public figures reflects lower standards in society.
   D Fewer people dare to contradict the opinions of other speakers.

5 The writer mentions 'the book' in line 61 as
   A an example of something else that people wrongly predicted would disappear.
   B the basis of the theory that people would soon stop talking to each other.
   C a way of introducing the works of famous writers from earlier centuries.
   D the source of information about the current state of political debate in the USA.

6 What point does the writer make in the final paragraph?
   A Nobody can escape the negative effects of the digital revolution.
   B Some traditional human values are eventually bound to disappear.
   C Everybody needs human contact whether they realise it or not.
   D Only those who remain polite and courteous will have friends.

3 READING AND USE OF ENGLISH

Idioms with *keep*

1 Read sentences 1–8. Match the idioms in italics with the meanings in the box.

> let someone know what's happening
> continue to know   try not to be noticed
> watch for someone to appear
> stop yourself smiling or laughing
> stay calm   hope things will turn out well
> do what they said they would

1 James promised to help me but he didn't *keep his word*.
2 Everyone else was shouting but somehow Nicole managed to *keep her cool*.
3 *Keep an eye out for* the waiter. If you see him, can you ask for the bill?
4 When people found out what Zoe had done, she *kept a low profile* for a while.
5 Is it ten already? I'm so busy I can't *keep track* of the time.
6 While I'm away you can *keep me posted* on events by email.
7 I *couldn't keep a straight face* when that boy claimed to be the world's best guitarist.
8 I'll *keep my fingers crossed* that you pass your driving test.

Part 4

> **Quick steps to Reading and Use of English Part 4**
> • Decide what part of speech the key word is, and what can go with it.
> • Think about what the question tests and all the changes you need to make.
> • Check you haven't left out or added any information.

2 Look at the example in the exam task. Answer these questions.

1 In the second sentence, how has 'constantly' changed? What part of speech follows it?
2 What change to 'attempted' is needed? Singular or plural?
3 Which idiom does 'profile' form? Is it positive or negative here?

3 Answer exam questions 1–6 using the clues in brackets (which don't appear in the exam).

Exam task

For questions **1–6**, complete the second sentence so that it has a similar meaning to the first sentence, using the word given. **Do not change the word given.** You must use between **three** and **six** words, including the word given. Here is an example (**0**).

Example:

0 Sam has constantly attempted not to attract attention since the trial began.

PROFILE

Sam has made constant ‾‾ATTEMPTS TO KEEP A LOW PROFILE‾‾ since the trial began.

1 The recent appearance of so many friendship websites online has been surprising.

SPRUNG (phrasal verb + adverb)

It's surprising that so many friendship websites ‾have recently sprung up‾ online.

2 Lisa threatened to resign if they did not increase her salary.

UNLESS (reporting structure with *that* + verb form with *unless*)

Lisa threatened that ‾she would unless‾ ^(they increed) her salary.

3 My internet connection was down so I wasn't able to follow events as they developed.

TRACK (structure following *prevent* + idiom)

My internet connection was down, which prevented ‾me from keeping‾ ~~track of~~ events as they developed.

4 Although Jake promised to continue to contact me, he never emailed me again.

TOUCH (noun + idiom)

Despite Jake's ‾promised to keep‾ ^(in touch) he never emailed me again.

5 'We're sorry we didn't keep our word,' the company said.

FOR (reporting verb and structure with *for* + pronoun)

The company ‾apologise for didn't keep their‾ word.

6 Defending himself against such a powerful opponent was a brave thing to do.

STAND (pronoun + three -part phrasal verb)

It was brave of ‾stand up to‾ such a powerful opponent.

> **Exam tip ›**
>
> Remember that contractions such as *I'd* count as two words, except *can't* (which is short for *cannot*).

3 SPEAKING

Asking for opinions, suggesting, and (dis)agreeing

1 Complete the expressions with the words in the box and then match them with a, b, c or d.

> along   feel   inclined   just   leave   move   point   thoughts

1 That's .... what I was thinking, too.
2 Let's .... that one for now.
3 I take your .... but ... .
4 How do you .... about this one?
5 Shall we .... on to the next one?
6 I'd go .... with you there.
7 What are your .... on this one?
8 I think I'd be more .... to ... .

a) asking for opinions
b) making suggestions
c) agreeing with someone
d) disagreeing politely

Part 3   **S** *Page 109*

Quick steps to Speaking Part 3
- Listen carefully to the instructions. Study the task for 15 seconds.
- Discuss each point fully before going on to the next one.
- Listen to what the examiner says after two minutes and prepare to make a decision.

2 Look quickly at the exam task instructions. What kind of things do you have to discuss?

3 🔵 1.09 Listen to students Leona and Mia practising this task. Answer these questions.

1 Do they spend about the same amount of time on each of the five factors?
2 Do they take turns and speak to each other politely?
3 Do they reach agreement on which factor has the most positive effect?

4 🔵 1.09 Listen again and answer the questions.

1 How do they begin the conversation?
2 Which expressions from Exercise 1 do they use?
3 Which other phrases do they use to express a–d?
4 How do they end the conversation?

5 Work in pairs. Read the first question and discuss the five factors for two minutes. Then read the second question and spend one minute deciding which factor to choose.

Exam task

Here are some things that can help make people's lives happy and a question for you to discuss. First you have some time to look at the task. Now, talk to each other about how important these factors might be in making individuals happy with their lives.

How important might these factors be in making individuals happy with their lives?

- Success in studies or at work
- Living a healthy lifestyle
- Perceiving beauty in nature and the arts
- Coping with life's problems as they arise
- Having good relationships with family and friends

Now you have about a minute to decide which factor has the most positive effect on human happiness.

6 Compare your decision with other pairs, giving reasons for your choice of most important factor.

Exam tip ❯

Adding to what your partner says, or politely disagreeing with them, will give you more to say than if you agree all the time!

3 WRITING

Register

1 Read texts A, B and C and answer the questions.

1. Which text is written in a formal style? Which is informal? Which is neutral, i.e. neither particularly formal nor informal?
2. Which of the following are used in each text?

a) phrasal verbs   b) long/less common words
c) exclamation marks   d) passive verb forms
e) impersonal expressions
f) conversational expressions
g) abbreviations   h) very short sentences
i) contracted forms   j) formal linking expressions

> **A**
> Sorry not to get back to you sooner. I've had a lot on, what with the new job and stuff like that. But we're in luck – I've just found out I've got the whole of next week off! So tell you what: let's get together Monday pm. Let me know asap if that's OK with you.

> **B**
> I am sorry it has taken me so long to reply to you, but I have been very busy because of my new job, among other things. Luckily, though, it seems I don't have to work next week, so perhaps we could we meet up after lunch on Monday? Please let me know as soon as you can if that would suit you.

> **C**
> I would like to express my apologies for the delay in replying to you. I have been extremely occupied on account of my new position, in addition to other matters. Fortunately, however, it has been announced that the office will be closed next week, which therefore means that I would able to meet you on Monday afternoon. I would be grateful if you could inform me as soon as possible whether that is convenient for you.

2 Replace the formal expressions in these grammatically correct sentences written by exam candidates with more neutral or informal words or phrases. Where might you see each of the formal expressions?

1. I was one of the persons in charge of the fund-raising.
2. I regret you couldn't come with us to the seaside. I missed you.
3. They'll give you training for the tasks you have to execute.
4. In my opinion it's better to awaken early, in time for breakfast.
5. I'll be waiting at the station, thus you'll be able to see me.
6. Nowadays, most families consume their dinner while watching TV.

Part 2: letter   W *Page 101*

3 Look at the exam task and answer these questions.

1. Is the letter extract formal, neutral or informal in style? Give examples.
2. Which sentence in the extract requires you to:
   a) ask for advice?   c) report a conversation?
   b) describe events?   d) give reasons?

Exam task

You are having problems with one of your flatmates and recently you mentioned it to your English-speaking penfriend. Here is part of a letter your penfriend sent you.

> So what exactly has your flatmate been doing – or not doing? Have you tried speaking to them? Why do you think they're behaving like that? I've got lots of experience of flat sharing, so is there anything I could give you a few tips on?

Write your **letter** in **220–260** words.

4 Quickly read the model letter on page 31. In which part of the letter does the writer do each of the following?

a) ask the reader for advice
b) give a reason for not replying quickly
c) report what was said
d) apologise for not replying quickly
e) ask the reader to reply quickly
f) describe the main events
g) thank the reader for their letter
h) answer the reader's question 'why'

5 How does the letter begin and end? How else can you begin and end informal letters and emails? Do these phrases go on a separate line or not?

6 Read the model letter again. Answer these questions.

1 What name does Lee give his penfriend?
2 What examples are there of a) informal language? b) neutral language?
3 Which reported speech forms does the writer use?
4 Find phrases in Lee's email that mean:

a) it's certainly not true   b) as well as all the other bad things   c) very late at night   d) talked to someone for a short time   e) so far   f) not make much difference   g) not wanted as a friend

Dear Ashley,

Thanks for your message – it's great to hear from you. And sorry not to get back to you until now, but I've been having a quiet weekend: out in the countryside!

Unfortunately, it's not been so relaxing at home. Far from it. Ever since he moved in, our new flatmate Charlie has refused to tidy up, left both the kitchen and the bathroom in a terrible state, and – to cap it all – has been keeping me awake until all hours with some of the worst music I've ever heard.

So the other week Jamie (my other flatmate) and I had a word with him. Charlie admitted he'd done almost no housework, said he was sorry and explained he hadn't actually flat-shared before. He promised he'd make more of an effort in future, though as yet our chat seems to have had little effect.

I got the impression he's a bit down. He clearly didn't want to talk about it, but I wouldn't be surprised if he's missing his family, both to talk to and to tidy up after him! I also wonder whether he's feeling slightly left out – Jamie and I get on really well, and three's rarely the ideal number.

So what I'd like to ask, firstly, is whether you think there might be something else that's bothering him, and also how we can make him see we want to be friends with him. And finally, how do you suggest we get him to turn the music down?

Hope to hear from you soon.

Best wishes

Lee

Quick steps to writing a Part 2 letter
- Carefully read the task and any text you are given.
- Decide who you are going to write to, why, and whether to use a formal, neutral or informal style.
- Note down points to include and put them under headings.
- Write your letter using a suitable paragraph layout, with the opening and closing on separate lines.

7 You are going to write your own letter. Look at this exam task and answer the questions.

1 Will your friend be with you? How does that affect the content?
2 Should you write in a formal, neutral or an informal style?
3 What points must you include?

Exam task

> This is part of a letter you have received from an English-speaking friend.
>
> Guess what! I'm spending next summer in your country, though sadly not in your town. I'm sure I'll enjoy my visit even though I don't speak the language very well – and I'm a bit shy, too. But I really want to make new friends, so please tell me: what are the best ways to meet people there, and **why**?
>
> Write your **letter** in **220–260** words.

8 Get ideas for your letter by using these prompts.

1 How old is your penfriend? Where will they be staying?
2 How could they be more confident speaking your language?
3 Why shouldn't they feel shy in your country?
4 Which of these would be good ways for them to meet people?
   - doing lessons at a language school
   - taking part in cultural or sports activities
   - exchanging language conversation
   - checking out websites for making friends
   - going to places where people of the same age hang out
5 For each of the points you chose in 4, note down at least one reason.

9 Plan your letter. You may want to organise your text like this:

Friendly greeting
Paragraph 1: thank the other person for writing
Paragraph 2: encourage them to speak your language and say why they needn't be shy.
Paragraph 3: ways of meeting people 1 with reasons
Paragraph 4: ways of meeting people 2 with reasons
Request a reply
Friendly close

10 Write your letter. When you have finished, check your work as in Unit 1, Writing Exercise 8 on page 15.

Exam tip ›

Don't copy the input material – use your own words.

Part 7

1 Discuss these questions in small groups.

- What are the advantages and disadvantages of running your own business?
- What kind of business, or other type of organisation, would you like to run? Why?

2 Look at the exam task. Quickly read the instructions, the introduction and the main text. Answer these questions.

   1 What is the writer's main purpose?
      A to warn others not to set up that kind of business
      B to advertise a particular product to readers
      C to give advice about setting up a small business
      D to show how recession affects small businesses
   2 In general, how is the article organised? How might this help you put some of the missing paragraphs in the right places?

> **Quick steps to Reading and Use of English Part 7**
> - Look for the development of an argument or narrative in the main text.
> - When you choose one of A–G, make sure it fits the overall structure of the text.
> - Check it for language links in the paragraphs both before and/or after the gap.

3 Do the exam task.

Exam task

You are going to read a newspaper article about young people setting up their own business. Six paragraphs have been removed from the article. Choose from the paragraphs **A–G** the one which fits each gap (**1–6**). There is one extra paragraph which you do not need to use.

Make your idea and start selling it

In a business environment where over 90 per cent of new products fail at launch, getting out there is the only way to truly understand your market, says Alex Neves, director of a ready-to-cook meals company.

At 3.45 a.m. on a rainy morning in May two years ago, I woke to a chorus of alarm clocks, and headed down to a street market in London to meet Phil, my school friend and business partner. On arriving there, I found him setting up the stall with our meal kits: boxes with all the fresh ingredients already chopped, washed and weighed.

> **1**   E

Neither of us had had any previous business experience. We had, though, followed the advice of countless start-up guides and new business seminars for those just starting out: we had written a business plan, identified market trends and developed a product.

> **2**   C

While this sort of research was invaluable, we were faced with a slight problem. On the basis of our research findings, we'd have 95 per cent of adults, across all socio-economic groups, buying our products at a cost of £6 per go, at least four nights a week – for all eternity.

> **3**   A

This gave us confidence that our plan was a good one. However, it also highlighted that maybe we'd missed something, that there were clearly some fundamental questions that hadn't been answered and couldn't be tested in this way: Was our product right? Would people actually buy it?

4 ✘ F

Fortunately, we landed on our feet, selling 100 meals on our first day of trading. And despite a few nail-biting initial hours after the market opened, our rather direct promotional activity (literally grabbing customers off the street) finally paid off. To our great delight, we sold out by the end of the day.

 5 ✘ B

The street market offered us a low-cost and flexible platform from which to start building up a record of sales. These proved essential in developing future sales, raising finance from banks and building up relationships with suppliers.

 6 D G

The most valuable aspect of our experience in the street market was that it allowed us to communicate with our customers on a daily basis and respond to their feedback on our products, marketing and pricing in real time. Over the three months, we were able to take many small-scale risks and experiment with many different recipes, points of sale and kinds of messaging, allowing us to develop those that worked and tweak those that proved unpopular.

A That, of course, excludes the extras they would buy for their close friends and family. Clearly, people were so taken with the idea that they would want to share it with others.

B Above and beyond the pleasing sales figures, the insights gained from that opening session were so useful that we kept our stall at Whitecross Street Market for three months. Looking back, we would not recommend any other approach to businesses that are launching products for the first time.

C Phil and I had also organised focus groups to try out early prototypes and set up an online questionnaire. We'd even pestered commuters in train stations to find out what they thought of the concept.

D How much this fairly low-budget advertising campaign achieved in terms of helping to boost sales is difficult to evaluate, not least because it proved impossible to determine what proportion of our customers had actually been influenced by it. All we can say with a fair degree of certainty is that the market research we carried out enabled us to identify the target audience pretty accurately.

E This was it. After months of painstaking planning, our task was simple: cast aside the books and theory, make up our products and get them into the kitchens of paying customers.

F This realisation, that the proof of the pudding is in the eating, led us to the 3.45 a.m. wake-up calls and a real drive to test our products on the paying public. We rented a stall at Whitecross Street Market, splashed out on a second-hand chiller, decorated our stall and made the tentative leap from business plan to business.

G It's amazing how much more seriously people in such crucial sectors take you when they can check out a product that is actually selling. Even if that is only in small quantities, rather than one that is only hypothetical.

4 Discuss the meanings of these expressions in the text.

market trends (para 2)	launching products (B)
promotional activity (para 5)	focus groups (C)
raising finance (para 6)	market research (D)
marketing and pricing (para 7)	target audience (D)
points of sale (para 7)	the paying public (F)

Phrasal verbs with *out*

5 Use the context to work out the meanings of these phrasal verbs.

get out (introduction)	try out (option C)
start out (para 2)	splash out on (option F)
sell out (para 5)	check out (option G)

6 Complete the sentences with phrasal verbs. Use the correct form of these verbs with *out*.

> back   bail   check   chill   cut   get   kick   run

1 After a hard day's work, I just like to chill out at home.
2 During the last recession, many small businesses ran out of money and had to close.
3 Let's check out that new café. I've heard it's not bad.
4 When news of a political crisis got out, the currency fell sharply on foreign exchange markets.
5 Despite their promises, the company back out of the deal when the economic situation worsened.
6 By cutting out meat, you can eat more healthily and save money.
7 A highly-paid player was kick out of the team for laziness.
8 One bank had such huge debts it had to be bail out by the government.

English langu
gram·ma
way the
constru
these
Englis
features

4 GRAMMAR

Passive forms Page 91

1 Rewrite the sentences in the passive using the words given. Then match them with uses a–f.

1 Next, they send you an email confirming your purchase.
Next, an ....

2 Somebody broke into the office last night.
The ....

3 A gang dressed as clowns held up the bank.
The bank ....

4 Sources have reported that the firm made a loss.
The firm *was reported* ....

5 People must always follow safety procedures.
Safety procedures ....

6 Many think that unemployment will rise.
It *'s sort out* ....

a) to state a rule or make a polite request
b) to indicate we don't know who did something
c) to describe part of a process
d) to emphasise the object rather than the subject
e) to say what people tend to expect, believe, etc.
f) to indicate we don't know who said something

2 In small groups, use passive verb forms to describe how each of the following works. There are some useful expressions in the box.

| basket bid cashpoint credit deduct |
| purchase receipt SIM card transaction |

Example: The card is placed in the machine, then the PIN number …

1 credit card
2 online shopping
3 pay-as-you-go mobile phone
4 internet auction site

Now use the form *It…* to say more about each.

Example: It is said to be the reason why so many people get into debt. It has been reported that thieves have copied cards.

Causatives:
have/get/want something done G Page 92

3 ⊙ Correct the mistakes in these sentences written by exam candidates. Then match them with uses a–c.

1 In the city centre, take care to have not your bicycle stolen.
2 We spent a lot on training and we don't want the money be wasted.
3 A car is expensive and costs money every time you get it to be repaired.

a) When we would like something to happen, or not happen.
b) When you arrange for someone else to do something for you. (*informal*)
c) When something bad is done to you or your possessions.

4 Reply to these questions using *have*, *get* or *want* + object + past participle.

Example: Have you finished writing that book? Yes, I hope to have it published next year.

1 Did you know the heel on one of your shoes is broken?
2 How would you like me to do your hair?
3 What did you tell the insurance company after the burglary?
4 If you were a millionaire, what would you have done for you?

5 Complete the second sentence so that it has a similar meaning to the first sentence. Use three to six words, including the word given.

1 My friend Steve fixed my old printer for me.
HAD
I .... my friend Steve.

2 It was a problem in the accounts office that delayed the payment.
HELD
The payment would have been made on time if *it hadn't been* .... by the *held* accounts office.

3 I want them to make me a smart new suit for the interview.
MADE
I *want ~ a smart new suit made* .... for the interview.

4 Economists believe that the rise in oil prices caused last year's downturn.
BELIEVED
Last year's downturn *it believed to* .... by the rise in oil prices. *has been cell*

5 Alfie never put any money in his account so the bank closed it.
HAD
Alfie *account had been* he never put any money in it. *accout closed because*

6 There were reliable reports yesterday that interest rates would rise soon.
REPORTED
It *was reliably* .... that interest rates would rise soon. *reported*

4 READING AND USE OF ENGLISH

Fixed phrases

1 Match the underlined C1-level phrases with the meanings in the box.

> for now but not permanently   as a type   except   forever
> in general   in the first place   more than anything else
> much less   in order to do something

1 Louise is saving up money <u>with a view to</u> buying a house.
2 Nathan has no income <u>other than</u> an allowance from his parents.   *except*
3 My dad rarely has a weekend off work, <u>let alone</u> a whole week.   *much less*
4 I don't want to go out. <u>For a start</u>, it's late. It's also cold.   *in the first place*
5 Occasionally you can get cheap concert tickets, but <u>by and large</u> they're quite expensive.   *in general*
6 This shop is <u>first and foremost</u> a food store, but it also sells household items.   *more than anything else*
7 Eleni and Georgios have split up <u>for good</u>. They've both got new partners now.   *forever*
8 My motorbike's off the road so <u>for the time being</u> I'm using buses.   *for now but not permanently*

2 Complete the sentences with your own ideas.

1 My parents are having their house repainted with a view to ....
2 I can't afford to buy a second-hand bike, let alone ....
3 It's a seaside town, so there are no industries other than ....
4 I need a new mobile phone, but for the time being ....
5 Although I've lived abroad for years, I remain first and foremost ....
6 There are still a few homes without a computer, but by and large *...computer*
7 I won't leave home for good until *...I get married*
8 I'm in no hurry to get married. For a start, *I'll go travel*

Part 2

Quick steps to Reading and Use of English Part 2
- Read the title and the text quickly for overall meaning.
- Fill in any words you're sure of.
- For the remaining gaps, look at the context and words around each gap.
- Check the completed text makes sense and is grammatically correct.

3 Quickly read the text, ignoring the gaps for now. Answer these questions.

1 What mistake has often been made about new technology?
2 What kind of invention is likely to succeed in the future?

4 The example answer (**0**) completes the fixed phrase *far from*. Think about the words that form fixed phrases with items 1, 4, 5 and 8 as you do the exam task.

Exam task

> For questions 1–8, read the test below and think of the word which best fits each gap. Use only **one** word in each gap. There is an example at the beginning (**0**).
>
> Example: **0** FAR
>
> ### Making money from inventions
>
> Making a fortune from an invention is (**0**) .... from easy. It is all (**1**) *all*.... predicting the technology of the future, (**2**) *which* has always been notoriously difficult. (**3**) *from* 19th century scientists ruling out the possibility of 'heavier-than-air flying machines', to information technology specialists convinced that home computing 'would never catch on', there is a long history (**4**) *of* people who should know better getting it completely wrong.
>
> By and (**5**) *........*, it is unwise to say that something will never happen, particularly in the fields of science and technology. How, in view of that, can present-day inventors get it right? The most successful innovations in the coming years (**6**) *are* predicted to be those for the home, above all technology that (**7**) *both* makes people's everyday lives easier and conserves scarce energy resources. Anyone who manages to think up a device which can do that (**8**) *may* well become very rich indeed.

Exam tip ❯

You never have to write contractions like *don't* or *we'd* in Part 2.

4 LISTENING

Money vocabulary

1 Explain the meanings of the underlined C1-level expressions.

1 The company will survive as long as it <u>breaks even</u>, but if it makes <u>a loss</u> it may go out of business.
2 <u>Affluent</u> people often have two large homes, whereas even a small flat may be <u>unaffordable</u> for the poor.
3 Customers whose accounts are <u>overdrawn</u> must pay 15% <u>interest</u> on money owed to the bank.
4 This was once a <u>prosperous</u> town, but since the recession many firms have gone <u>bankrupt</u>.
5 If you're <u>well-off</u> you can afford to save each month but if not, you'll find it hard to <u>make ends meet</u>.
6 The <u>gross</u> income of an average worker is currently <u>taxed</u> at a rate of 25%.
7 You can make a small <u>saving</u> on socks in that shop, but don't buy T-shirts there. They're a real <u>rip-off.</u>
8 The firm doesn't have enough <u>funds</u> to repair the damage, but the insurance will <u>cover</u> it.

Part 3

Exam tip >

Don't choose an option until the speaker has finished talking about that point.

2 Discuss these questions, using expressions from Exercise 1 where possible.

1 When young people go away to study, where does their income come from and what are their outgoings?
2 Why do some get into financial difficulties and how can they resolve them?

Quick steps to Listening Part 3
- Read the instructions for information about the speaker.
- Underline the key words in the first line of each question. They help you focus on what you need to listen for.
- Choose the option that expresses the same idea as what you hear: you won't hear exactly the same words.

3 🔘 1.10 Underline the key words in the first line of each question, e.g. *choice, account* in question 1. Then listen and do the exam task.

Exam task

You will hear an interview with a student called Liam, who talks about the financial difficulties he faced during his first year at university. For questions **1–6**, choose the answer (**A, B, C** or **D**) which fits best according to what you hear.

1 Liam's <u>choice</u> of bank <u>account</u> was based on
  A the availability of interest-free overdrafts.
  B the gift from the bank to new student customers.
  C the location of the nearest branch of the bank.
  D the high credit limit on credit cards for students.

2 Liam believes the most useful student discounts are for
  A travelling by rail.
  B going to the cinema.
  C eating out.
  D online shopping.

3 Following the theft of his laptop, Liam wished he had
  A taken his possessions with him during the vacation.
  B thought about the need for insurance cover.
  C made sure his room on campus was more secure.
  D used a stronger password to protect his data.

4 Liam was surprised to discover how much he had been spending on
  A social activities.
  B loan repayments.
  C clothes shopping.
  D taxi fares.

5 When he got into debt, Liam felt
  A confident he could deal with the situation on his own.
  B annoyed that nobody had warned him that could happen.
  C unconcerned as he knew his parents would help him.
  D apprehensive about what the lenders might do next.

6 What advice does Liam give to others who are in debt?
  A Take out a longer-term loan to pay off the immediate debt.
  B Spend nothing until you have saved enough to clear the debt.
  C Set up a regular repayment plan for a fixed period of time.
  D Negotiate a lower interest rate with those you owe money to.

4 SPEAKING

Expressing opinions

1 Complete each expression. In some cases more than one answer is possible.

1 My own .... is (that) …
2 From my .... of view, …
3 It .... to me (that) …
4 The way I .... it, …
5 To be perfectly .... , …
6 As far as I .... …
7 I'm inclined to .... that…
8 To .... mind, …

Part 4 S *Page 111*

Quick steps to Speaking Part 4
- Listen carefully to the instructions because they are not written down.
- If you have no particular views on the subject, quote other people, e.g. *Some people say …*
- Give reasons and examples.
- Add to your partner's ideas and/or encourage them to say more.

2 🔘 **1.11** Listen to Esra and Stefan, two strong exam candidates, practising Part 4. Who expresses these opinions? Write E, S or B (for *both*) next to each.

1 When they leave the family home, everyone has to learn how to manage money.
2 Financial independence can be risky for young people from poorer families.
3 The governments of rich countries should spend more on overseas aid.
4 Governments and charities should provide aid for poorer countries.
5 A lot of rich people are unhappy.
6 Some people would be happier if they had more money.

3 🔘 **1.11** Listen again. Note down the expressions Esra and Stefan use to justify their opinions, e.g. *The main reason is … .*

4 Work in groups of three. Do Part 4 three times, choosing different questions from the list.

When it is your turn to be the examiner:
- ask the others three questions, prompting if necessary with *Why?* or *Why not?*
- make sure they both answer, by asking *What do you think?* or *Do you agree?*
- stop them after five minutes and tell them how well you think they did the task.

List of questions for Speaking Part 4

1 Some people find it very difficult to get out of debt. Why do you think this is?
2 Do you think electronic means of payment will ever completely replace cash?
3 How much do you think people need to earn to live comfortably?
4 Do you think schools should teach children how to manage money?
5 What are the advantages and disadvantages of having a credit card?
6 Do you think today's society places too much importance on making money?
7 How important do you think it is to save for the future?
8 How much income tax do you think very rich people should pay?
9 How far do you agree with the statement 'the best things in life are free'?

Exam tip ›

Remember it is your English that is being tested, not your ideas – there are no 'right' or 'wrong' answers.

4 WRITING

Addition links

1 The linking expressions below are used at the beginning of sentences and paragraphs to introduce points in a certain order. Put them into the correct groups below.

a) above all b) additionally c) as well as that
d) besides e) finally f) firstly g) for a start h) furthermore
i) in addition j) in the first place k) last but not least l) lastly
m) more importantly n) most importantly o) moreover
p) on top of that q) secondly r) to begin with s) what's more
t) worse still

For the initial point: ....
For subsequent points: ....
For the last point: ....

Which three of those used for subsequent points are quite formal, and which two are fairly informal?

2 Ask yourself the questions about each of the advertisements below. Then use your answers to write a paragraph about one of the ads. Link your points with expressions from Exercise 1.

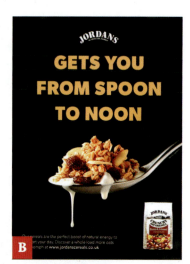

	A	B
1 Does it attract your attention?	☐	☐
2 Is it aimed at a particular type of person?	☐	☐
3 Does it tell you anything new?	☐	☐
4 Is its message simple?	☐	☐
5 Does it promote the name of the brand?	☐	☐
6 Does it highlight the product's benefits?	☐	☐
7 Is it believable?	☐	☐
8 Does it make you want to do something now?	☐	☐

Part 1: essay   *Page 99*

3 Look at the exam task instructions and notes. Answer these questions.

1 What do you have to write about, and for whom?
2 Which areas must you write about?
3 What can you also include?

Exam task

Write your answer in **220–260** words in an appropriate style. Your class has been watching a TV documentary about the impact of advertising on society. You have made the notes below.

> ### Areas affected by advertising
> - our everyday lives
> - what we buy
> - the economy

> Some opinions expressed in the discussion:
>
> "Some of the ads on TV are really funny."
>
> "It makes people spend money on things they don't really need."
>
> "A lot of people work in advertising companies."

Write an essay for your tutor discussing the effects on two of the areas in your notes. You should explain which area you think is affected more and provide reasons to support your opinion. You may, if you wish, make use of the opinions expressed in the discussion, but you should use your own words as far as possible.

4 Example paragraphs A, B and C all deal with the first point in the exam task, i.e. how advertising affects our everyday lives. Read them and answer these questions.

1 Each paragraph looks at the effects of advertising on our everyday lives. Which discusses a) the positive effects b) the negative effects c) both?
2 Which paragraphs use one of the handwritten opinions? How has each writer rephrased it?
3 Find a) addition links b) contrast links c) passive verb forms.

Firstly, the advertising industry employs a lot of people to make their products looks prettier than other companies whose make consumer familiar with and trust their brand.
Secondly, they have widely employees to do different jobs such as employees who take videos and photos for the promoting package. Telc or employees who have skills to develop the movie better publishing to the public

A

We are surrounded nowadays by advertising, and although some television adverts might make us smile, most of it is an unwanted intrusion. To begin with, there are the huge, often ugly billboards in public places. Then there are those irritating little online ads popping up while you work, and when you get home you are met by a pile of junk mail. Worse still, the radio seems to keep playing the same annoying ads all day long.

B

It has been said that advertising is the greatest art form of this century and there is some truth in that, even if it can at times appear tasteless and materialistic. Firstly, the high technical standards in visual advertising have launched the careers of many top photographers and film directors. In addition, it is very much part of popular culture in its use of fashion, music and celebrities. Above all, it can help change attitudes by challenging stereotypes and reflecting the diversity of modern society.

C

Advertising is seen by some as one of modern society's evils. It makes us greedy, they say, targeting even young children with its consumerist message. Furthermore, it constantly interrupts our television programmes, blocks up our email inboxes and wastes our time with unsolicited phone calls. On the other hand, some advertisements are visually beautiful, others make you think and a few can make you laugh out loud. Moreover, some are truly memorable: almost everyone can recall their favourite TV ad from childhood.

Advertising is the business of trying to persuade people to buy products or services, and it has increasingly profound and wide-ranging effects on present-day society. The effects on consumer preferences and on the economy in general are particularly significant.

It is difficult to evaluate the influence of advertising campaigns on consumer choice, but it must be substantial or companies would not spend so much on them. Firstly, they inform people about new products, special offers and so forth. In addition, they increase demand by showing brands being used by people like you – or by people you want to be like. This may, however, indicate that consumers are being sold unnecessary items. Secondly, some advertising works subconsciously, so people don't even know why they are choosing particular brands.

Moreover, Advertising would inform their product's proportion or any special deal, which might increase demand of consumer.

Advertising is a major industry. Besides employing thousands of people itself, it stimulates demand for products which in turn leads to higher production and more jobs. What is more, the revenues it generates help support newspapers, television channels and even top football clubs. Advertising, though, is expensive, and ultimately the cost is passed on to the consumer. Also, the large salaries it pays attract some of the country's brightest and most creative young people, who could otherwise be employed in more productive or socially useful sectors.

they also try to persuade the consumer by using a famous person who you like. There has too been advertisement everywhere since the signs on the street to the building board of electronic devices, which they would have reference to consumer behaviour.

My own view is that the biggest effect of advertising is on the economy, as it creates employment both directly and indirectly. Its influence on what people choose, conversely, may have been exaggerated, especially as nowadays more objective sources of information about products are available online.

However, sometimes they exaggerate the product by own advertising which might have consumer buying those unnecessary product

6 You are going to do the exam task. To help you get ideas, discuss these questions with your partner and make notes.

1 Which of the points in the model essay and in the example paragraphs in Exercise 4 do you agree with? Which do you disagree with?
2 Are internet ads more, or less, effective than TV ads?
3 Do successful ads make people buy things immediately?
4 Are people more or less likely to buy a product if a celebrity recommends it?
5 Do some ads promote harmful things by giving them a glamorous image?
6 Why do songs used in ads sometimes become popular?

5 Read the following model essay and answer the questions.

1 What is the purpose of the opening paragraph?
2 Which two of the notes does the writer use, and where?
3 Which of the handwritten opinions does he use, and how does he rephrase them?
4 Which area does he think is affected more by advertising and what reasons does he give?
5 What addition links and contrast links does he use?
6 What passive forms does the essay contain?
7 Where does he give his own opinion and what expression does he use to introduce this?

> **Quick steps to writing a Part 1 essay**
> - If the intended reader is your tutor, write in a fairly formal style.
> - Discuss issues in a balanced way, including points for and against.
> - Connect your points with addition links.

7 Look at the Quick steps, then plan and write your essay. After finishing, check your work as in Unit 1, Writing Exercise 8 on page 15.

> **Exam tip >**
>
> Try to use different words from those in the handwritten comments, e.g. *unaffordable* instead of *too expensive*.

Word building

1 Work in small groups. Fill in the missing parts of speech in the table.

Verb	Noun	Adjective	Adverb
	medicine/medic		
	surgery/surgeon		
prevent			
treat			
prescribe			
infect			
		conscious	
	clinic/clinician		

2 Look at the pictures and answer these questions.

1 What does each person's job consist of?
2 Which of those jobs would you like to do and which wouldn't you like to do? Why?

Part 2

Quick steps to Listening Part 2
• Underline the key words in the questions.
• Decide what kind of information, e.g. a place, you need.
• Listen for ideas similar to the key words.

3 Look at the exam task. Which question(s) focus(es) on:

• types of people?   • a school subject?
• places?   • a physical object?
• abstract ideas?

4 🔘 **1.12** Do the exam task. For each question, listen for the kind of information you identified in Exercise 3.

Exam task

You will hear a woman called Lin Cheng talking about becoming a medical student.

For questions 1–8, complete the sentences with a word or short phrase.

As a child, Lin was told by her (1) ~~parents~~ ~~friend~~ ~~classmate~~ that she should take up medicine as career.

Lin believes the school underestimated her (2) academic ~~ability~~ ~~progress~~ .

Lin was not very good at (3) ~~science~~ Maths so she decided against studying information technology.

At the medical centre, Lin observed a form of (4) ~~researcher~~ ~~job satisfaction~~ which is unique to a career in medicine.

Lin felt frustrated by her lack of (5) medical knowledge while working at the nursing home.

Lin found talking to (6) ~~medical~~ students the most rewarding aspect of her visits to medical schools.

Receiving the (7) ~~accepted~~ ~~from~~ letter is something Lin says she will always remember.

Lin's long-term aim is to treat patients in (8) ~~local~~ ~~hospital~~ ~~developing~~ ~~in country~~

Exam tip ▷

When you hear an answer, write what you hear. Don't try to use your own words.

5 GRAMMAR

Conditional forms   G *Page 93*

1 Look at the Grammar Reference on page 93 and then match three of the endings with each sentence. Why is the other one not possible?

1 If you'd drunk more water,
A you'd have felt a lot better.
B you'd feel a lot better.
C you'd be feeling a lot better.
D you'd felt a lot better.

2 Carl would have taken longer to recover
A if he had not been so fit.
B if he might not have been so fit.
C if he were not so fit.
D had he not been so fit.

3 The surgeon will operate on you
A provided you sign this form.
B on condition that you sign this form.
C if you will sign this form.
D supposing you sign this form.

4 This medicine is safe
A   as long as you don't exceed the stated dose.
B unless you exceed the stated dose.
C in case you don't exceed the stated dose.
D assuming you don't exceed the stated dose.

5 Others would have caught the disease
A provided that he had been carrying it.
B if he were carrying it.
C had he been carrying it.
D if he had been carrying it.

6 It'd be best to call the health centre
A if you feel dizzy again.
B providing you feel dizzy again.
C should you feel dizzy again.
D were you to feel dizzy again.

2 ⊙ Correct the mistakes in these sentences written by exam candidates. Use conditional forms without *if*.

1 Holidays are good for us under the condition that we are relaxed.

2 I am ready to accept your offer unless you take into account my remarks about the plan.

3 If I had children, they would be free and independent as long as they prove to be trustworthy and responsible.

4 Had there been more computers available, the users had more time for other activities.

5 I am extremely grateful were you to allow me to make some small changes to the schedule.

6 It is not dangerous for someone to drive a car, in case that he or she follows the rules.

3 Complete the second sentence so that it has a similar meaning to the first.

1 Tyler is feeling ill because he ate too much.
Tyler wouldn't ....

2 I'll call the nurse if your temperature doesn't go down.
Unless ....

3 Emma became a doctor because she is a caring person.
If Emma ....

4 You will only lose weight if you do plenty of exercise.
Provided ....

5 Mr Kay didn't know he was unwell so he carried on working.
Had ....

6 Patients are usually treated in one day, but not if surgery is required.
As long as ....

7 What will Eva's children do if she has to go into hospital?
Supposing ....

8 Please inform the receptionist if you need a further appointment.
Should ....

9 To buy medication on this website you must have a prescription.
On condition ....

10 Paramedics will treat minor injuries if there are any accidents.
Were ....

4 Use conditional forms to discuss the following in pairs.

1 Things you would have done differently if you had known then what you know now.
2 What your life would be like now if certain things had or hadn't happened.
3 What conditions you would attach to making major changes in your life, e.g. choosing a university, getting a job, moving abroad, buying a house, forming a relationship.

5 READING AND USE OF ENGLISH

Part 8

1 How dangerous do you think each of these sports is? Complete the table with the names of the sports in the pictures.

Sport	Number of injuries per 1,000 hours of activity
1 Rugby	30
2 Basketball	14
3 Running	11
4 Skiing	8
5 Tennis	5

2 Which parts of the body do the sports people above risk injuring? Use some of these words:

> dislocate   fracture   sprain   tear   twist   aches
> blisters   bruises   soreness   swelling

3 How can sportspeople prevent these injuries?

4 Look quickly at the exam task instructions, then at the title and introduction to the text. What kind of text is it and what is it about?

5 Read the questions, underlining the key words as in question 1. Which questions focus on the same ideas you had in Exercise 3?

6 Look at the Quick steps and do the exam task.

> **Quick steps to Reading and Use of English Part 8**
> • Underline the key words in each question.
> • Scan each part of the text for words or phrases that express the same ideas as the key words.
> • Underline the parts of the text that provide the answers.

Exam task

You are going to read a magazine article in which five athletes give advice on avoiding injuries. For questions **1–10,** choose from the sections (**A–E**). The sections may be chosen more than once.

Which athlete makes the following statements?

The <u>average</u> runner is likely to suffer at least <u>one injury</u> every <u>twelve months.</u>	1	D
There is <u>no evidence</u> that doing other sports helps <u>runners avoid injury.</u>	2	C
Building up <u>muscle</u> can help prevent injury.	3	A
<u>Stretching</u> prior to running has <u>no beneficial</u> effects.	4	C
At the <u>beginning</u> of a <u>training</u> programme, don't try to do <u>too much</u> too soon.	5	D
The kind of <u>surface</u> you run on makes <u>little difference</u> to the risk of injury.	6	A
<u>Avoid speeding up</u> right at <u>the end</u> of a run.	7	E
It is advisable to do some <u>gentle exercise</u> just after you <u>finish running.</u>	8	B
The biggest <u>risk</u> comes from <u>not having</u> adequate <u>breaks</u> from training.	9	E
<u>Pain</u> does <u>not</u> always mean you must <u>stop</u> <u>training</u> immediately.	10	B

> **Exam tip ▶**
>
> Remember that the answers in the text are not in the same order as the questions.

Avoiding injuries

What can athletes do to prevent injuries occurring? Five experienced runners give some advice.

Athlete A

Wearing the correct running shoes is essential if injury is to be avoided. However, the shock transmitted through the body when running on different types of ground hardly varies at all, as the athlete subconsciously adjusts the stiffness of their leg according to whether their foot is about to land on tarmac, track or grass. Even so, it makes sense to reduce the degree of foot impact, and therefore the danger of stress injuries, by diversifying one's general fitness training. This could include cycling and swimming, while weight training has a role to play in this respect by strengthening the body and thereby improving posture and balance. Needless to say, such training should cease at the slightest sign of any discomfort.

Athlete D

As a runner, the odds are against you remaining injury-free for a full year, and those odds shorten dramatically if you fail to allow sufficient time for your body to recover between sessions, whether they be workouts, training or racing. Second only to that as a risk factor is being over-ambitious in terms of what you can reasonably hope to achieve when taking up serious running. Everyone likes to win and there's no harm in finishing a race strongly, but try to progress step by step at first. At the first sign of any pain or discomfort, take note of what your body is telling you and stop running straightaway.

Athlete B

Pain, of course, can be a warning sign of impending injury, and many coaching manuals warn of the dire consequences should an athlete be so foolish as to try to run through it. In severe cases that warning undoubtedly makes sense, but I would take issue with it regarding milder conditions such as muscle soreness that are an inevitable by-product of a hard workout. To minimise post-training discomfort, I'd always make a point of doing a little cooling-down work such as stretching. It also makes sense to cross-train, to strike a balance between running and other disciplines like cycling and rowing, both of which have the advantage of providing relief from the constant pavement pounding which must surely have a harmful effect on marathon runners, above all.

Athlete E

Over the two and a half years I've been running, I've only had one physical problem severe enough to force a reduction in training, which from what I can gather is about average. To be blunt, I've never really seen the point of so-called preventative measures such as gradually increasing running speeds when you're starting out, or taking regular breaks from training. I suppose the only exceptions are stretching, which everyone seems to agree is essential, and maintaining an even pace while running, on the grounds that finishing strongly may feel empowering, but that is precisely when your running is at its most erratic and your muscles are at their most susceptible to strains and tears.

Athlete C

Research shows that the key to preventing injuries occurring is to learn how to run injury-free rather than cross-train, which in fact involves practising movement patterns that have nothing at all in common with running. In some cases, such as weightlifting, cross-training activities can actually cause other kinds of damage that can set a runner's training programme back weeks or even months. Conventional wisdom also has it that pre-exercise stretching lowers the risk, whereas studies comparing the incidence of lower-limb injuries among those who stretch before training and those who don't show no difference whatsoever. Stretching at other times, such as in the evening, does seem to reduce injury risk, although there are probably more effective ways of doing so, for instance by habitually training on soft surfaces.

7 Find C1-level phrases in the text which mean the following.

a) as you would expect (A)
b) disagree (B)
c) make certain I always do (B)
d) give the same amount of attention (B)
e) important thing in (achieving something) (C)
f) what most people believe (C)

g) none at all (C)
h) it is unlikely (D)
i) one stage at a time (D)
j) pay attention to (D)
k) because of a particular reason (E)

5 READING AND USE OF ENGLISH

Suffixes

1 Answer these questions about each of the C1-level words in the box.

1 What part of speech is it? e.g. comparable – *adjective*,
2 What suffix does it have? e.g. *-able*,
3 What word is it formed from? e.g. *compare*
4 Are there any other spelling changes to that word? e.g. *drops final 'e'*
5 What part of speech is that word? e.g. *verb*

> ~~comparable~~ competence inevitably leadership
> participant pointless qualification skilful
> specific statistical summarise threaten

2 👁 Correct the mistakes in these sentences written by exam candidates.

1 Like in many other countries, life in the city here is hectic and stressing.
2 Modern machinery and facilities would help the factory immensly.
3 Old, unuseful sports equipment should be given away.
4 The only inconvenient is that generally you can't find a place near the stadium to park.
5 The organisers are very apologising about cancelling tomorrow's race.
6 I think the government should subsidies people like musicians, artists and actors.
7 The aim of this proposal is to state my views about the culture event.
8 And they all lived happy ever after.

Part 3

> **Quick steps to Reading and Use of English Part 3**
> • Decide what changes you need to make, e.g. noun to verb.
> • Check your spelling, especially when adding a suffix.
> • Make sure your completed text makes sense and is grammatically correct.

3 Look at the exam task instructions and quickly read the text. Why, according to the author, is the use of modern sports technology sometimes unfair?

4 Look at the example (0). What change in part of speech is made? What suffix is added?

5 Do the exam task. Note changes to the parts of speech.

> **Exam tip** ›
>
> Remember you have to change _all_ eight words in capitals. Don't leave any unchanged!

Exam task

For questions **1–8**, read the text below. Use the word given in capitals at the end of some of the lines to form a word that fits in the gap **in the same line**. There is an example at the beginning (0).

Example: 0 SUBSTANTIAL

Technology in sport

In certain Olympic sports, there has been a **(0)** .... increase in speeds in recent Games. This has been particularly **(1)** .... in cycling, for instance, leading to questions about how much of the vastly improved **(2)** .... is the result of better training and fitter athletes, and how much of it is down to **(3)** .... advances such as the use of lighter materials in bike manufacture. Some would argue that the constant **(4)** .... of sports technology is just as important as the ongoing improvements in training methods, making the sport more exciting for **(5)** .... and spectators alike. For this to be fair, however, it assumes the **(6)** .... of the new equipment to all the competing athletes, which for **(7)** .... reasons is unlikely to be the case for some. In everyday situations a saving of just 0.01 seconds may sound **(8)** .... , but in an Olympic context, where the result can be decided by thousandths of a second, it can make all the difference between winning and losing.

SUBSTANCE

NOTICE

PERFORM

TECHNOLOGY

EVOLVE

PARTICIPATE

AVAILABLE

ECONOMY

SIGNIFY

5 SPEAKING

Compound adjectives

1 Form compound adjectives by matching words from Box A with those in Box B and adding a hyphen, e.g. *cross-country*.

A

| cross fair first friendly full high |
| highly left long record twenty world |

B

| breaking country distance famous |
| haired handed kilometre length |
| looking qualified rate risk |

Now think of more compound adjectives using one word from each compound, e.g. *cross-cultural*.

2 Complete the sentences. Use compound nouns formed from the words in the boxes in Exercise 1.

1 In that picture there's a tall woman wearing a hat and a short, ... man.

2 It looks like a .... race, probably a marathon because they're on a city street.

3 She's a .... woman, but I'm sure she's also a tough competitor.

4 It's a .... Olympic swimming pool, which measures 50 metres.

5 That's the .... Maracana stadium in Rio de Janeiro. Everybody's heard of it.

6 Some say hang gliding is a .... sport, but it's quite safe if you're careful.

3 Form compound adjectives using each of these words. Explain the meaning of each.

hard- open- one- short-

Part 2   *Page 108*

Quick steps to Speaking Part 2

- During the other candidate's long turn, listen without interrupting.
- Be ready to comment on the pictures when he or she has finished.
- Listen to the examiner's question and talk for up to 30 seconds.

4 ⏺ **1.13** Read the Quick steps and the exam task instructions. Then listen to Zeinab and Reza doing Part 2 and answer these questions.

1 Which two photos does Zeinab compare?
2 Does she do both parts of the task?
3 Does Reza speak for about the right length of time?

5 ⏺ **1.14** Listen again to Reza and answer the questions.

1 What expression does Reza use to ask the examiner to repeat the question?
2 Who does he think has put the most effort into acquiring their skills?
3 What reason does he give for his answer?

6 Work in pairs and do the exam task using pictures 1 and 2. Then change roles and do the task using pictures 2 and 3.

Exam tip ❯

The question you answer about your partner's pictures is not written down, so ask the examiner to repeat it if you are not clear what you have to do.

Exam task

Each of you will be given three pictures. You have to talk about **two** of them on your own for about a minute, and also to answer a question briefly about your partner's pictures.

Candidate A, it's your turn first. Here are your pictures. They show people winning Olympic medals. Compare **two** of the pictures, and say how difficult it might have been for them to acquire the skills needed to reach this level, and how those people might be feeling.

Candidate B, who do you think has put the most effort into acquiring their skills? Why?

> How difficult might it have been for them to acquire the skills needed to reach this level?
>
> How might these people be feeling?

7 Tell your partner how well you think you both did the Part 2 task, including the comments on your partner's pictures.

5 WRITING

Purpose links

1 In each sentence, underline the <u>two</u> expressions in italics which are possible.

1 We should lower admission fees <u>to</u> / *in order that* / <u>*in order to*</u> sell more tickets.

2 I bought a new TV (*so*) (*so that*) / *so as* I could watch the World Cup on a big screen.

3 The stadium is being rebuilt <u>*in order that*</u> / *in order to* / <u>*so that*</u> more spectators can be accommodated.

4 The town needs more facilities, *in order to* / *so* / *so as to* cater for a wider variety of sports.

5 I wore protection when I was boxing <u>*so that I wouldn't*</u> / *to not* / <u>*in order not to*</u> get hurt.

6 *So* / <u>*So as to*</u> / <u>*To*</u> ensure fairness, there is a limit on the size and weight of baseball bats.

7 It is important to keep to the footpaths, *in order to not* / <u>*so as not to*</u> / <u>*in order that you do not*</u> disturb the wildlife.

8 Some people take up sports like golf *so that* / <u>*in order to*</u> / <u>*so as*</u> to make new friends.

2 Using purpose links, tell your partner why some people take up the following sports and hobbies.

Example: aerobics – *so as to improve their level of fitness*

astronomy	drawing
hiking	martial arts
Pilates	pottery
Salsa dancing	scuba diving
vegetable gardening	Yoga

Part 2: proposal   *Page 104*

> **Exam tip >**
>
> If you use headings in your proposal, try to use different words from those in the exam task instructions.

3 Answer the questions about the exam task below.

1 What is the topic of the proposal?
2 Who are you writing for and why do they want a proposal?
3 What style should you write in?
4 Which main points must you include?

Exam task

You see this notice in a local newspaper of the town where you are studying English.

> The Government has promised our town a grant to invest in new sports facilities. The Planning Director invites you, as a resident or visitor, to send a proposal saying which sport should receive the money, how it should be spent and why it would benefit people in the town.

Write your **proposal** in **220–260** words in an appropriate style.

4 Quickly read the model proposal on page 47. Match these headings with the paragraphs. Which relates to each of the main points you identified in Exercise 3?

A sensible investment   Improving people's lives   The missing sport

Proposal for new sports facilities

Introduction

The aim of this proposal is to suggest the most suitable way of spending the government grant for new sports facilities.

1 *The missing sport*

This town already has extensive facilities for football, rugby and athletics, as well as an Olympic-size swimming pool and a top-class sports centre catering for a wide range of sporting activities. However, one increasingly-popular sport is conspicuous by its absence: squash.

2 *A sensible investment*

The grant would be spent on constructing a number of squash courts. To do this would not be overly expensive as the surface area needed would be small compared with tennis courts, for instance. Apart from the installation of a glass wall at the front of each so that matches can be watched from outside, no further expenditure would be necessary as squash players provide their own equipment.

3 *Improving people's live*

Squash is one of the most physically demanding of all sports, providing intensive exercise for up to four people over a short period of time. As courts would be in constant use from early morning to late evening, they would be a highly efficient way of raising many people's fitness levels. Moreover, it is likely that players would set up a lively social club, thereby strengthening the sense of community in the town.

Conclusion

I would strongly recommend that squash be chosen. It would be the most cost-effective way of spending the money and also the ideal way to improve people's quality of life.

5 Look at the model proposal again and answer the questions.

1 Where and how does the writer
a) state the purpose of the proposal?
b) make a recommendation?

2 Which verb tense does the writer use to talk about the future? Why?

3 Find examples of the following:
a) purpose links
b) compound adjectives
c) addition links

6 Look at the exam task instructions and answer the questions in Exercise 3 about it.

Exam task

You see this notice in the college where you are studying English.

> The Students' Association wants to increase the number of clubs at the college. Some of these clubs will cater for students' hobbies. Please write a proposal suggesting why your favourite hobby should be included and justifying its inclusion.

Write your **proposal** in **220–260** words in an appropriate style.

7 Discuss these questions in small groups.

1 Which is your favourite hobby and what does it consist of?
2 Does it need any special facilities or equipment?
3 What might other people like about it if they took it up?

8 Look at the Quick steps and plan your proposal.

Quick steps to writing a Part 2 proposal
- Make notes on the topic and on the arguments you will use.
- Organise your text clearly into paragraphs, using headings if you wish.
- Use a neutral or fairly formal style if the proposal is for an organisation, tutor or boss.
- State the purpose of your proposal in the first paragraph.
- Aim to persuade the reader(s) to accept your suggestions.

9 Write your proposal. When you have finished, check your work as in Unit 1, Writing Exercise 8 on page 15.

3 What are the advantages and disadvantages of seeing art and music: **a)** live? **b)** on TV? **c)** via the Internet?

Part 5

Quick steps to Reading and Use of English Part 5
- Look at the title and introduction, then quickly read the text.
- Remember that the questions follow the order of the information in the text.
- If an answer isn't obvious, cross out the options that are definitely wrong and choose from those remaining.

4 Read the text quickly. Which of the points you discussed in Exercise 3 does the writer mention?

5 For each exam question:

1 study the question or unfinished sentence
2 find the relevant part of the text
3 draw a vertical line next to it, plus the question number.

6 Do the exam task.

Exam tip ›

Remember you can answer the questions without understanding every word or phrase in the text.

Exam task

You are going to read a newspaper article. For questions **1–6**, choose the answer (**A, B, C** or **D**) which you think fits best according to the text.

Collocations

1 Which of these adverbs collocate with each adjective?

Example: generally / highly / widely acclaimed

Adverbs
absolutely completely deeply dreadfully
eagerly generally highly perfectly totally
utterly wonderfully widely

Adjectives
~~acclaimed~~ anticipated appalling distinctive
enjoyable hilarious imaginative overrated
pointless talented tedious unconventional

2 Say how you feel about each of the pictures using collocations from Exercise 1.

Online arts: Click-fix culture

You can watch a rock concert and tour an art gallery from the comfort of your armchair. But can it replace the thrill of the real thing? Fiona Sturges finds out

Fancy an evening at the theatre but can't face sitting there for hours? Theatre companies will happily stream performances live. Want to see a band but put off by the exorbitant ticket prices? No worries. Many mainstream bands allow their concerts to be streamed free of charge. Now galleries are getting in on the act too, enabling sofa-bound art lovers to wander around the world's greatest art institutions, all in high resolution and without fear of getting sore feet. But is it really the same as seeing paintings in the flesh? I decided to find out.

My first stop is the Uffizi in Florence, where I am immediately deposited in front of Botticelli's fifteenth-century *Birth of Venus.* In technological terms, it's very impressive. I can see every bump and line in the surface of the paint. If I were there in person, I would need one hefty magnifying glass to view it like this. It occurs to me that Botticelli would never have seen it in such detail and I wonder what he would have thought of us all marvelling at every sliver of paint through an online high-resolution prism.

Next, I head to the Museo Reina Sofia in Madrid, one of my favourite galleries. I enjoy myself racing past sculptures and going eyeball to eyeball with assorted portraits in a manner that would be frowned upon were I actually there. There's a lot to be said for viewing art this way. Admission is free and there aren't any queues. Plus, you won't have to listen to the babble of fellow visitors as they loudly broadcast their knowledge of surrealism.

But it's no substitute for the real thing. Billions of pixels can't accurately transmit the scale or colour or atmosphere of a painting or convey the sense of wonder you feel when standing in front of it. And only in a gallery do you have the opportunity to shut out the rest of the world, engage with a work and view it in context. My enduring thought, while strolling around the Reina Sofia online, is how much nicer it would be if I were actually in Madrid.

So how about a gig instead? If any medium has fearlessly embraced new technology it's pop, so the streamed concert is surely live music's logical evolution. Without leaving my postcode, I watch an outdoor music festival famous for its overcrowding. My initial feeling is of smugness as I get the best views of the best bands without the physical discomfort. But as the show goes on my attention starts to drift and I wander off to make a cup of tea.

Filmed concerts, whether on television or online, invariably struggle to convey the tension of live performance. That sensation of a crowd collectively holding their breath as a song reaches its crescendo – you don't get that sitting at home. Watching a band this way can be lonely too. I've got strong feelings about other people at pop concerts, notably those who sing along too loudly or photograph every moment with their mobile phones. But I'd sooner experience live music in a roomful of strangers than be standing there alone.

Art in almost all its forms is meant to be a communal experience. It is also a ritual, one that is about so much more than the cultural event itself. These are pilgrimages made by people in pursuit of a particular visceral sensation. Often the pleasure is as much in the anticipation as the execution. Remove the build-up, the tantalising bit where you imagine how it will be, and you take away a vital part of the experience.   *line 51*

Lying on the sofa, with computers, phones and remote controls all within easy reach, is my default setting. But when it comes to art appreciation, even a slob like me can recognise the basic requirement to leave the house. Ultimately it's a bit like watching holidays on telly. Yes, you can cut out the sweat, the aching legs, the ravenous mosquitoes and the dodgy souvenirs. By staying at home, you can take in the finest views. But it's just not the same if you can't feel the sun on your face.

1   What point is the writer making about *Birth of Venus* in the second paragraph?
   A   Modern technology reveals the flaws in the painter's technique.
   B   The painting lacks interest when seen over the Internet.
   C   She enjoyed it more when she actually went to the art gallery.
   D   We can examine it more closely than the artist himself could.

2   What, according to the writer, is a disadvantage of going to an art gallery in person?
   A   There is a risk of being disturbed by people trying to show off.
   B   It is impossible to concentrate on paintings because of distractions.
   C   You may be tempted to spend more time seeing the city than the gallery.
   D   There are often too many paintings of famous people from the past.

3   How does the writer react to seeing a concert online?
   A   She is glad to avoid the tense atmosphere at the event.
   B   She likes being able to have a drink while she watches.
   C   She enjoys the experience at first but then loses interest.
   D   She feels music has adapted too slowly to modern technology.

4   What does the writer say she enjoys about live music?
   A   taking photos of the concert
   B   forming part of the audience
   C   joining in with the songs
   D   watching the concert with friends

5   The word 'it' in line 51 refers to
   A   looking forward to the main event
   B   experiencing the actual performance
   C   observing other people enjoying art forms
   D   sharing the experience of travelling to the venue

6   The writer compares online art with holidays on television to show that
   A   appreciating art is more relaxing than going on holiday.
   B   art appreciation is less popular than watching TV.
   C   art cannot be fully appreciated from a distance.
   D   to appreciate art it is best to see it in sunny countries.

6 GRAMMAR

Verbs followed by the infinitive and/or -ing

G *Page 93*

1 Complete the sentences with the correct form of the verb in brackets. Then match each of the verbs in bold with a–f.

1 The security guards **caught** a thief .... (attempt) to steal a painting.
2 Anna's parents **should** .... (let) her have music lessons if she wants them.
3 I couldn't **afford** .... (go) to the ballet.
4 I **love** .... (listen) to blues or jazz.
5 I **wouldn't mind** .... (see) that band live.
6 My friends **persuaded** me .... (join) a theatre group.

a) infinitive without *to*
b) *to*-infinitive
c) object + *to*-infinitive
d) *-ing*
e) object + *-ing*
f) *to*-infinitive or *-ing* (with similar meanings)

Now add more verbs to each of categories a–f. Write an example sentence using one verb in each category.

2 Complete the sentences using the correct form of a suitable verb. Add an object where necessary.

1 To become a top musician, you have to practise
....

2 If tickets keep going up, people should refuse
....

3 In the cinemas, they shouldn't let
....

4 If you miss the start of the film, it isn't worth
....

5 When an artist sees lovely countryside, it can inspire
....

6 He once got into a rock concert by pretending
....

7 At first I couldn't see my friends, but then I spotted
....

8 If you have a backstage pass at a concert, it enables
....

3 Match the sentence halves and explain the difference in meaning when the verb is followed by *to* + infinitive or *-ing*.

1 a) I **meant** to see the exhibition
   b) Seeing the exhibition **meant**

   i) paying a lot to go in.
   ii) but it cost too much to go in.

2 a) We **tried** to play the song faster
   b) We **tried** playing the song faster

   i) but we found we couldn't.
   ii) but it sounded even worse.

3 a) I'll never **forget** taking
   b) I'll never **forget** to take

   i) those photos on my phone.
   ii) my phone with me again.

4 a) I **remembered** to get tickets
   b) I **remembered** getting tickets

   i) for the show and feeling so excited.
   ii) for the show, fortunately.

5 a) I **regret** to say that
   b) I **regret** saying that

   i) your application has been unsuccessful.
   ii) I didn't want to be in the band.

6 a) The star **stopped** talking to the journalist
   b) The star **stopped** to talk to the journalist

   i) standing near the red carpet.
   ii) who had misquoted her.

4 ⊙ Which of these exam candidates' sentences contain mistakes with verbs followed by the infinitive or *-ing*? Correct any mistakes.

1 I want that everything goes well next weekend.
2 I feel like to watch television.
3 The longer and the better the boy played, the more people stopped to listen to his music.
4 She wanted to be successful, even if it meant to postpone their wedding for a few years.
5 You have to remember doing exercise every day if you want to be healthy.
6 The fact we could communicate in English enabled us to hold really interesting debates.
7 You will get into trouble if you go on to behave like that.
8 When I saw how good the film festival was, I really regretted to not invite you.

6 READING AND USE OF ENGLISH

Frequently confused words

1 Complete the sentences with the best answers, A, B, C or D. Think carefully about the meaning of each word.

1 The print edition of the dictionary is regularly .... to include new words.
   A renovated
   B renewed
   C upgraded
   D updated

2 The sculpture is worth an .... $10 million.
   A assessed
   B evaluated
   C appreciated
   D estimated

3 The .... buildings in town are nearly a thousand years old.
   A historic
   B outdated
   C elderly
   D historical

4 The soloist .... her success on a series of acclaimed concerts.
   A assembled
   B built
   C composed
   D manufactured

5 My sister .... most of her spare time to writing poems.
   A assigns
   B devotes
   C allocates
   D distributes

6 At first .... , they look like photos, but they're actually drawings.
   A glimpse
   B view
   C gaze
   D glance

Part 1

Quick steps to Reading and Use of English Part 1

• For each gap, decide what part of speech the four options are.
• Before you look at the options, think of a word that might fit the gap.
• Cross out any options you are sure are wrong, and choose from those that remain.

2 Quickly read the title and the text in the exam task. What is the writer's overall purpose?

3 Look at each question and decide what part of speech the options are, e.g. 0 *verbs*.

4 Do the exam task.

> **Exam tip** ›
>
> Look at the whole sentence before choosing an option.

Exam task

For questions **1–8**, read the text below and decide which answer (**A, B, C** or **D**) best fits each gap. There is an example at the beginning (**0**).

Example: 0 A urges **B** stimulates **C** persuades **D** encourages

CONTEMPORARY ART MATTERS

Contemporary art plays on the emotions and **(0)** ....B.... the mind. It can send powerful messages, **(1)** .... political, social or environmental issues. It can also lead to **(2)** .... reactions, including outrage from those who like to be shocked.

It is available to everybody. Admission to contemporary art museums is usually free, whereas viewing traditional art often **(3)** .... going to expensive art galleries to see the **(4)** ....

Major museums may contain thousands of works, and although inevitably some will not be to everyone's **(5)** .... , many will be quite fascinating. They may even **(6)** .... the visitor to create their own pieces; if not for display in a museum, then as a form of street art – which is a wonderful way for young people to **(7)** .... their feelings and ideas.

In fact, creating works of contemporary art can be therapeutic, often proving **(8)** .... effective in helping people recover from emotional or psychological problems.

	A		B		C		D	
1	rising		focusing		highlighting		concentrating
2	hard		strong		high		deep
3	obliges		forces		makes		means
4	extracts		exposures		exhibits		exploitations
5	taste		fancy		appetite		flavour
6	affect		inspire		impress		influence
7	inform		comment		account		express
8	highly		utterly		perfectly		absolutely

6 LISTENING

1 Discuss these questions.

    1 Why do people go to see collections like those in the pictures?

    2 Which do you find most/least interesting? Why?

Part 4

Quick steps to Listening Part 4
- Look quickly at both tasks to see what you have to listen for in each case, e.g. *problems*, *opinions*.
- Listen to everything a speaker says before deciding on an answer.
- At the end, check that you have chosen an answer for all the questions.

2 Look quickly at the exam task. Which part of this particular task, Task One or Task Two, focuses on the speakers' feelings, and which on the context?

3 Note down:
- words associated with each of the activities in Task 1.
- words or phrases with similar meanings to the adjectives in Task 2.

4 🔘 **2.02** Do the exam task. Listen for the words you noted down in Exercise 3, and for the same ideas expressed in different words.

Exam task

You will hear five short extracts in which people describe cultural activities.

While you listen you must complete both tasks.

TASK ONE

For questions **1–5**, choose from the list (**A–H**) the activity each speaker is describing.

    A watching a DVD at home
    B going to the opera
    C going to the theatre
    D listening to a concert on the radio
    E viewing an exhibition of posters
    F going to the cinema
    G visiting a museum of ancient artefacts
    H viewing a collection of photographs

Speaker 1   C   **1**
Speaker 2   A   **2**
Speaker 3   E   **3**
Speaker 4   **4**
Speaker 5   **5**

TASK TWO

For questions **6–10**, choose from the list (**A–H**) how each speaker says they felt during the activity.

    A disappointed
    B puzzled
    C bored
    D fascinated
    E scared
    F amused
    G depressed
    H angry

Speaker 1   B   **6**
Speaker 2   A   **7**
Speaker 3   D   **8**
Speaker 4   G   **9**
Speaker 5   A   **10**

Exam tip ⟩

Remember that you may hear answers to Task Two before answers to Task One.

Expressing likes, dislikes & preferences

1 🔊 **2.03** Complete the dialogue with these words. Then listen to check your answers.

> appeal   dislike   favourite   keen   mind   nothing
> prefer   preference   rather   stand

Kim: There's (1) _nothing_ ...... I like more on a Saturday evening than watching that talent show.

Abbie: I can't say it's one of my (2) _favourite_ ...... programmes. If I'm at home then, my own (3) _preference_ ...... is for a good historical drama.

Kim: They don't really (4) _appeal_ ...... to me, to be honest. I'd much (5) _rather_ ...... see a good crime series.

Abbie: Really? I'm not at all (6) _keen_ ...... on those. They all seem the same to me. And there's far too much violence – I really can't (7) ...... that.

Kim: Not in all of them. From what you say, you'd probably (8) _stand_ ...... the ones that show actual murders, but I don't think you'd (9) ...... the kind of detective series that I enjoy.

Abbie: Maybe, but I still think I'd (10) _prefer_ ...... to watch *Downton Abbey*.

2 Which of these expressions in the box are followed by:

a) the bare infinitive?
b) the *to*-infinitive
c) *-ing*?
d) either the *to*-infinitive or *-ing*?

> would rather   keen on   can't stand   dislike
> don't mind   prefer   would prefer   enjoy   hate

3 For 1–6, say what you like and dislike about each, then say which you prefer. Use a range of expressions from Exercise 1.

1 contemporary art / traditional art
2 cinema / theatre
3 ballet / opera
4 classical music / pop music
5 folk music / jazz
6 rap & hip hop / rock

Part 1 🅢 *Page 107*

> **Quick steps to Speaking Part 1**
> - Be friendly and polite to the other candidate and the examiners.
> - Speak clearly and loudly enough for both examiners to hear you.
> - If you are asked about your likes or preferences, try to use a range of expressions.

4 🔊 **2.04** Listen to these extracts from Olga and Nikos practising Part 1. Assess their speaking using the five points in Exercise 4 on page 13 [Unit 1].

5 🔊 **2.04** Listen again. Which expressions do they use to express likes, dislikes and preferences? What would you add to their comments?

6 Work in groups of three: one 'examiner' and two 'candidates'. The examiner asks each candidate some of these questions. The examiner then comments and makes suggestions.

1 What kind of TV programmes do you like, and which do you dislike?
2 Do you prefer to listen to music on your own or with friends?
3 What do you enjoy most about being on holiday?
4 Do you prefer to spend your free time at home or going out with friends?
5 What kind of books do you enjoy reading?
6 Do you prefer to watch one episode of a series at a time on TV, or lots of episodes together on DVD?
7 What do you like most about spending an evening in a big city?
8 Do you prefer watching films made in your country or those from other countries?

Exam tip ❯

When you reply to a Part 1 question, look at the examiner – not the other candidate.

6 WRITING

Praising and criticising

1 Decide which of the adjectives in the box below are used to praise, and which to criticise. Then add an adverb to intensify each adjective.

Example: action packed – to praise, incredibly action-packed

action-packed brutal far-fetched gloomy
gripping moving powerful predictable
pretentious slow-moving spectacular
stylish subtle unconvincing uninspired
witty

2 Note down three films or TV series you would recommend, and three you wouldn't.

Tell your partner about them using the expressions in the box plus the *to*-infinitive or *-ing*.

Give reasons using phrases from Exercise 1.

Example: I would definitely recommend watching this series. It is totally convincing and extremely powerful.

I would definitely (not) recommend …
My advice is (not) …
I would advise against …
Viewers would be well advised (not) …
This series is certainly (not) worth …

Part 2: review *Page 105*

3 Discuss these questions with a partner.

1 What kind of things are reviewed in newspapers, magazines and online?
2 What do you expect to find in a review?
3 How far would you be influenced by a good or bad review of a film or TV series?

4 Look at the exam task and answer the questions.

1 What do you have to review?
2 Who are you writing for and why do they want a review?
3 What must you do in your review?

Exam task

You see this notice on a film review website.

In every imaginable category there are so many great films to watch, both old and new. The trouble is, there just isn't time to see all of them. So to help film lovers make informed choices, we regularly post reviews comparing and contrasting movies. Send us your review of two films of a similar type of any age, together with your recommendations, and we may well post it on our site.

Write your **review**.

5 Quickly read the model review on page 55 and answer the questions.

1 Did the reviewer enjoy watching
a) *Goldfinger*   b) *Skyfall?*
2 Which does the reviewer particularly recommend?

Two must-see Bond movies

Skyfall, directed by Sam Mendes, is a massively-popular action film featuring secret agent James Bond. Just as, almost fifty years earlier, Guy Hamilton's *Goldfinger* was, too.

In the older film, Bond has to prevent aptly-named gold smuggler Auric Goldfinger from stealing the US gold reserves in Fort Knox, following narrow escapes from death in England and Switzerland. In *Skyfall* it is the Secret Service itself, in particular Bond's boss M, that is under attack. The action takes place in superbly-shot locations as far apart as Istanbul and Macau, Shanghai and Scotland, as 007 battles Javier Bardem's utterly evil Silva.

These frequent changes of setting help maintain the pace of both films, holding the viewer's attention throughout – as do the highly-accomplished actors who play Bond. Other similarities include the magnificent title songs, sung by Shirley Bassey and Adele respectively, that famous suspense-building incidental music, and even the same Aston Martin car. In both movies, Bond faces genuinely scary opponents, particularly Goldfinger's deadly assistant Oddjob, although *Skyfall* keeps the excitement level a little higher by having longer action sequences.

One key difference is that *Skyfall*'s M is a woman, brilliantly played by Judi Dench. This, unfortunately, does not reflect any real change in the role of female characters in Bond films, even after half a century. Another criticism is the amount of violence, often shown in rather unnecessary close-up.

To sum up, both films are certainly worth watching, but for today's audience, accustomed to the non-stop action of movies like *Mission Impossible*, I would probably recommend *Skyfall*.

6 Answer the questions about the model review.

1 In which paragraph(s) does the writer:
- give a synopsis of each film?
- make recommendations?
- give a little background information?
- mention characters in both films?
- aim to catch the reader's attention?
- criticise both films?
- praise both films?

2 According to the reviewer, what similarities are there between the films? What contrasts are there?
3 What examples are there of adverb/adjective collocations?
4 What style is the review written in?
5 What expressions give the reviewer's own opinions?
6 Does the review make you want to watch either of the films (again)?

Quick steps to writing a Part 2 review
- Choose a subject for your review and decide if you enjoyed it.
- Think about what your readers will want to know.
- Plan your review, ensuring it contains description, praise and/or criticism and a conclusion.
- Sound enthusiastic if you enjoyed what you are reviewing.
- End either by recommending or advising readers against the subject.
- Give your review an eye-catching title.

7 Look at these exam task instructions and answer the questions in Exercise 4 about it.

Exam task

You see this announcement in an international magazine called *Home Entertainment*.

Nowadays there are so many box sets of TV series on sale in the shops and online that it can be difficult to know which to choose. Our reviews section aims to help people make those choices. We therefore invite readers to send in a review comparing and contrasting two different TV series.

Write your **review**.

8 Discuss these questions in small groups.

1 What is your favourite type of TV series?
2 Which two series of that type made most impression on you? Why?

9 Look at the Quick steps and plan your review. For each series, make notes about some of these:

- the type of series
- the setting(s) and plot
- the main characters
- the acting
- the soundtrack
- the photography
- themes, e.g. bravery, dishonesty
- who it might appeal to

10 Write your **review** in 220–260 words in an appropriate style. When you have finished, check your work as in Unit 1, Writing Exercise 8 on page 15.

Exam tip ›

If you have to review two different things, write a similar amount about each.

7 Green issues
LISTENING

Collocations

1 Look at the pictures and discuss the questions in pairs.

   1 Where do you think these photos were taken?
   2 Which would you most like to visit?

2 🔘 **2.05** Match the words in box A with those in B to form collocations. Then listen to the recorded text to check your answers.

A

| carbon climate drought endangered become forest |
| fossil global habitat melting rainforest rising |

fossil fuel *carbon emission* *climate change* *global warming*
B   *melting* *icecaps*   *rising sealevel*
                                        forest fire

| | | *become extinct* | | |
| fuels emissions clearance warming fires change |
| icecaps conditions destruction sea-levels species |
| extinct |

drought condition *habitat destruction*

3 Look at each picture again. Answer the questions using expressions from Exercise 2.

   1 How important is this kind of area to the Earth's climate and wildlife?
   2 What kind of dangers does it face, and what might happen if it is not protected?

> **Exam tip** ›
> Make sure you know which extract you are listening to.

Quick steps to Listening Part 1
- Read each introduction and first line of the questions.
- Think about who will be speaking, why, and about what.
- Don't choose an answer before hearing the whole extract.

Part 1

4 Look at the exam task and answer these questions.

   1 Which extract relates to which picture?
   2 Who will you hear and what will they talk about?
   3 What are the key words in each question?

5 🔘 **2.06** Listen and do the exam task.

Exam task

You will hear three different extracts. For questions **1–6**, choose the answer (**A**, **B** or **C**) which fits best according to what you hear. There are two questions for each extract.

Extract One

You overhear two colleagues talking about the man's recent holiday.

   1 What does the man complain about?
      A the cost of accommodation
      B the lack of snow
      C the large crowds

   2 How does the woman react to what he says?
      A She is concerned about the implications.
      B She is not convinced he is telling the truth.
      C She is sympathetic about the problem he had.

Extract Two

You hear two friends discussing a documentary programme about a tropical rainforest.

   3 They agree that
      A the commentary was irritating at times.
      B the photography was of poor quality.
      C the programme was too short.

   4 The man says the programme seemed to have been made
      A in Australia.
      B by amateurs.
      C on a low budget.

Extract Three

You hear part of an interview with a woman called Anne Murphy, who is campaigning against the building of a new factory.

   5 Anne is opposed to the plan because
      A there is no need for additional jobs in the district.
      B the river could become polluted by waste.
      C the infrastructure would have to be upgraded.

   6 What would Anne prefer instead of the current plan?
      A turning the land into a leisure facility
      B leaving the fields exactly as they are now
      C building a smaller factory in the same place

7 GRAMMAR

Inversion of subject and verb G *Page 94*

1 👁 Most of these sentences written by exam candidates are correct, but five contain errors. Correct any mistakes. Then answer questions a–f about the expressions in bold.

1 **Seldom** have I seen such a determined person.
2 **Little** did the children know they were in for so many adventures together in the future.
3 **Only when** they start performing they *will they* discover any hidden talents they might have.
4 **Not until** the 20th century did travelling become a widespread phenomenon.
5 **Never before** Sonia *had* had ever had such a feeling of freedom and strength.
6 **Under no circumstances** we *can we* can allow this kind of accident to happen again.
7 **On no account** should we assume our planet will always provide us with enough food.
8 **Hardly** had he finished the sentence, when the telephone rang.
9 **At no time** when she was in Paris was Carlota really aware of her true feelings.
10 **No sooner** did *had* he finish his studies than he decided to become a wildlife photographer.
11 **Nowhere** else in the world will you find this strange-sounding but lovely bird.
12 **Not only** *do* private cars contribute to this chaos in our cities, they also pollute the air.

a) What kinds of adverbial expression require inversion of subject and verb?
b) Where in the sentence do these expressions usually go?
c) How does inversion affect the way a sentence sounds?
d) How does the word order change when there is an auxiliary verb?
e) What is added when there is no auxiliary verb?
f) When would you use sentences like these?

2 Rewrite the sentences by putting the words in *italics* at the beginning and making any other necessary changes.

1 It was *only when* we arrived in Kenya *did we see* that we saw hippos and giraffes.
2 I'd *hardly* *hardly had I* unpacked in my hotel room when my phone rang.
3 The nature reserve guards *seldom* catch illegal hunters.
4 I have *never before* *had I seen* seen such a spectacular waterfall.
5 There are *no longer* *are there any* any tigers in the northern region.
6 The zebras had *no sooner* *had the* entered the water than hungry crocodiles appeared.
7 Visitors to the forest must *on no* *must* *on no account* light fires.
8 The local people are *in no way* *are* to blame for the destruction of the forest. *In on way are the local people*

3 Make these sentences more emphatic by using inversion forms from Exercises 1 and 2.

1 This is the longest drought there has ever been.
2 We had little idea of what would happen when darkness fell.
3 There won't be any chance of rescuing survivors until the storm has passed.
4 Visitors are not permitted to leave the designated footpaths, for any reason.
5 There are bears and also wolves in those hills.
6 Wild flowers started to appear as soon as the rains came.
7 It is rare to see fish in a river as polluted as this.
8 The climbers set off for the summit and almost immediately it began to snow.

4 Imagine you have to do these writing tasks. For each task, write three sentences using the expressions given.

1 A list of safely rules for people visiting a safari park.
   On no account ....
   At no time ....
   Under no circumstances ....
2 A narrative about an adventure you had.
   Hardly ....
   No sooner ....
   Little ....
3 A description of a beautiful part of your country.
   Nowhere else ....
   Rarely ....
   In no other country ....
4 An account of events in your country's history.
   Not until ....
   Only when ....
   Not since ....

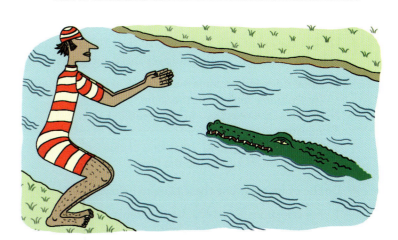

7 READING AND USE OF ENGLISH

Part 7

1 Compare the pictures using some of these expressions.

> commuters   congestion   fuel consumption   gridlock
> car horns   car occupancy   jams   rush hour   smog
> exhaust fumes

2 Discuss these questions.

1 Is traffic getting better or worse where you live? Why?
2 In which parts of the world do you think it is getting much worse? Why?
3 The amount of traffic in some cities is actually reducing. What reasons can you think of for this?

> **Quick steps to Reading and Use of English Part 7**
> • Fill in any gaps you are sure about first.
> • Don't leave any gaps blank.
> • At the end, make sure the option left over does not fit any of the gaps.

3 Look at the exam task. Quickly read the title, the main text and options A–G, then answer these questions.

1 What does *motormania* mean? Look at the introduction for a phrase that means the same.
2 Which of the reasons you discussed in Exercise 2 question 3 are mentioned?
3 What kind of text is it? What kind of clues, therefore, should you look for to do the task?

4 Do the exam task. Use these clues to help you.

1 For questions 1, 3, 4 & 6, find reference words and phrases with similar meanings.
2 For question 2, look for the previous *explanation(s)*.
3 For question 3, also look for an addition link.
4 For question 5, find an addition link and a contrast link.

Exam task

You are going to read a newspaper article about changes in car usage. Six paragraphs have been removed from the article. Choose from the paragraphs A–G the one which fits each gap (1–6). There is one extra paragraph which you do not need to use.

The end of the road for motormania

Something unexpected is happening to our car-crazy culture. What are the forces driving us out of motoring?

Is the west falling out of love with the car? For environmentalists it seems an impossible dream, but it is happening. While baby boomers and those with young families may carry on using four wheels, a combination of our ageing societies and a new attitude among the young seems to be breaking our 20th-century car addiction. Somewhere along the road, we reached the high point of the car and are now cruising down the other side.

1	F

The phenomenon was first recognised in *The Road... Less Traveled*, a 2008 report by the Brookings Institution in Washington DC, but had been going on largely unnoticed for years. Japan reached it in the 1990s. They talk there of "demotorisation". The west had its tipping point in 2004. That year the US, UK, Germany, France, Australia and Sweden all saw the start of a decline in the number of kilometres the average person travelled in a car that continues today.

2	B

Demographics are another possible explanation. It is surely no accident that 'peak car' happened first in Japan, which has the world's oldest population. Pensioners do not drive to work, and many don't drive at all. There is also the rise of "virtual commuters" who work from home via the Internet.

3	A G

Social scientists detect a new 'culture of urbanism'. The stylish way to live these days is in inner-city apartments, not the suburbs. Richard Florida, an urban studies theorist at the University of Toronto in Canada, points out that the young shop online, telecommute, live in walkable city neighbourhoods near public transport and rely more on social media and less on face-to-face visiting. Given those changes, they can think of better ways to spend their money than buying a car.

4	C A

The industrialised world still has plenty of less-green trends too. Falling car occupancy is one. In the US, the average car on the average journey carries 1.7 people, half a person less than in 1970. So even if we individually travel less, our cars may travel just as much.

5	E

But the good news is that those straight lines on the planners' graphs predicting ever rising car-kilometres and ever-worsening carbon emissions from internal combustion engines are being proved wrong. Meanwhile, the use of everything else, from bikes and buses to trains and trams, is unexpectedly going up.

6	C D

Some think car use will revive if and when economies recover. But it looks like something more profound is going on. Florida calls it a "great reset" in society that will have profound consequences – not least for the environment. Even our most treasured consumer aspirations can have a peak. Enough can be enough.

Exam tip 〉

Highlight the language links you find so that you don't waste time looking for them again.

A   Of course, environmentalists shouldn't get carried away with all this. In the developing world, the car boom is only now getting under way, despite gridlock in cities from Shanghai to São Paulo. That trend makes any claim of an impending global peak in car usage far-fetched.

B   What could be driving us off the road? Fuel costs and rising insurance premiums may be a factor. And urban gridlock, combined with an absence of parking places and congestion charging, makes an increasing number of us look on the car as a dumb way to move around in cities where there are public transport alternatives.

C   Planners need to take note of these miscalculations. And, if they have any sense, they will start to reinforce these trends with improved public transport, an end to urban sprawl and more investment in inner cities.

D   In the US, similarly, the decline of the car among the young is most dramatic not in the gridlocked city centres but in the car-dependent suburbs. In sprawling cities like Atlanta and Houston where the automobile is king, driving is down by more than ten per cent.

E   Likewise, by insisting on driving bigger and more powerful cars we are wiping out the gains from more fuel-efficient vehicles. And sometimes we simply replace driving with flying.

F   That peak takes several forms. Sales of new cars have almost halved in the US, down from nearly 11 million in 1985 to about 5.5 million now. We shouldn't take much notice of that, though. Cars last longer these days, and sales go up and down with the economy. But we have hit peak car ownership, too. And, more to the point, peak per-capita travel.

G   Besides these new employment patterns, leisure lifestyles are also changing. The biggest fall in car use in the US is among people under 35. The fraction of American 17-year-olds with a driver's licence has fallen from about three-quarters to about half since 1998. Twenty-somethings have recently gone from driving more than the average to driving less.

5   Use the context to work out the meanings of these phrasal verbs. What other meaning can each have?

1   carry on (1st paragraph)
2   go on (2nd paragraph)
3   rely on (4th paragraph)
4   look on (option B)
5   insist on (option E)

7 SPEAKING

Phrasal verbs with *on*

1 Complete the sentences using phrasal verbs with *on*. Choose from these verbs in the box.

call	catch	come	draw	move	run	stay	take

1 After the party had ended, I *stay on* to help tidy up.
2 The report *call on* research carried out in several countries.
3 If electric cars *take on* with the public, the air will be much cleaner.
4 Marko is looking tired. I think he's *catch on* too much work.
5 If that light *come on*, it means you're running out of petrol.
6 Environmentalists have *draw on* the Government to finance green projects.
7 This device *run on* rechargeable batteries.
8 OK, we've discussed that picture, so let's *move on* to the next one.

Giving examples

2 🔊 **2.07** Fill in each gap with one suitable word, then listen to check your answers.

Environmentalists are calling on all of us to recognise that waste is fast becoming a major problem. (1) .... at the amount we throw out every year. A family of three, (2) .... , produces more than a ton of rubbish every year, and this is steadily rising. A case in (3) .... is plastic, used in ever greater quantities and often ending up in the bin. An obvious (4) .... of this is the plastic shopping bag. Also, (5) .... paper waste. Did you know that every year the average family throws out the equivalent of six trees?

3 Discuss the problem of waste creation in society, giving some of these points as examples.

- the good food that is thrown out
- the old electronic devices that become hazardous waste
- the cars and other vehicles that are broken up
- the rubbish that goes into landfills
- the garbage that is burnt
- the rivers and seas that are polluted

Part 3 **S** *Page 109*

Quick steps to Speaking Part 3
- Begin by saying something like *Shall we start with this one?* or *Do you want to go first or shall I?*
- Take turns with your partner throughout.
- Consider both the positive and the negative aspects of each prompt.

4 Look quickly at the exam task instructions. What do you have to talk about?

Exam task

Here are some ways we can reduce the amount of waste we create and a question for you to discuss. First you have some time to look at the task. Now, talk to each other about how effective these suggestions might be in reducing the amount of waste we create.

How effective might these suggestions be in reducing the amount of waste we create?

- Recycle as much rubbish as possible
- Give away unwanted clothes
- Buy products that have little or no packaging
- Read online versions of newspapers and magazines
- Buy only as much food as you need

Now you have about a minute to decide which suggestion would be most effective in reducing the amount of waste we create.

5 🔊 **2.08** Listen to this extract from Aishar and Haziq practising Speaking Part 3. Answer these questions.

1 Which prompt are they discussing?
2 Which student sounds less confident at first?

6 🔊 **2.08** Listen again. What questions and phrases does Aishar use to encourage Haziq to speak and feel more confident?

7 Look at the Quick steps and Exam tip, then do both parts of the exam task in pairs. Help your partner if necessary.

8 Compare your decision with other pairs, saying which suggestion you chose and why.

Exam tip ›

Avoid spending too long talking about one of the prompts. Remember, you need to discuss them all.

7 READING AND USE OF ENGLISH

Idioms: nature

1 Match these idioms with their meanings. Are any of them similar in your first language?

1 play with fire
2 down to earth
3 over the moon
4 out of the blue
5 a drop in the ocean
6 a breath of fresh air
7 the tip of the iceberg
8 keep your head above water

a a small part of a big problem
b new, different and exciting
c completely unexpectedly
d tiny amount compared to what is needed
e have just enough money to live on
f take a foolish risk
g delighted about something
h sensible and practical

2 Complete the sentences with idioms from Exercise 1.

1 Frieda was .... when she passed her music exam.
2 Creating a new virus in the laboratory is an example of scientists ....
3 It isn't easy .... when you're living on a student's income.
4 One person using solar energy is .... but if everyone does so it'll make a difference.
5 I hadn't heard from Jody in years, but .... I had an email from him.
6 Lee's ideas are fine in theory but don't work in practice. Selma, though, is far more ....
7 So far we've only found a few trees with the disease, but sadly they're likely to be ....
8 After so many years at school, I'm finding life at university is ....

Part 4

> **Quick steps to Reading and Use of English Part 4**
> • Look for any other changes you need to make, e.g. adjective to adverb.
> • Make sure your answer fits the words both before and after the gap.
> • Write no more than six words and no fewer than three.

3 Look quickly at the exam task. Which questions mainly test: a) a phrasal verb? b) an idiom? c) inversion of subject and verb?

Example: 0 *idiom*

4 Do the exam task.

Exam task

For questions **1–6**, complete the second sentence so that it has a similar meaning to the first sentence, using the word given. **Do not change the word given.** You must use between **three** and **six** words, including the word given. Here is an example (**0**).

Example:

0 The government's announcement of investment in tidal energy came as a complete surprise.
   BLUE
   The government _ANNOUNCED OUT OF THE BLUE_ that there would be investment in tidal energy.

1 Immediately after the storm began, lightning struck the roof.
   SOONER
   No .... lightning struck the roof.

2 There seems little chance of paper shopping bags becoming popular with consumers.
   ON
   Paper shopping bags seem unlikely .... consumers.

3 Visitors are not allowed to approach the animals in the Reserve, for whatever reason.
   SHOULD
   Under no .... the animals in the Reserve.

4 Alone in that small boat, I had no idea what time it was any more.
   TRACK
   Alone in that small boat, I had completely .... time.

5 Those trucks cause air pollution and they make a terrible noise, too.
   ONLY
   Not .... the air, they make a terrible noise, too.

6 Ollie's attempt to make his in-laws feel relaxed by telling a joke was not a success.
   ICE
   Ollie tried ...., ... with his in-laws by telling a joke.

> **Exam tip** ▶
>
> Sometimes more than one answer is possible, but you must only give one of them.

7 WRITING

Sentence adverbs

1 We can use an adverb, often at the beginning of the sentence followed by a comma to show how we feel about the fact or event we are writing about. Replace the *underlined* words in the following sentences with adverbs in the box.

> admittedly apparently fortunately
> generally happily mysteriously
> obviously sadly unexpectedly
> unsurprisingly

1 Last winter was one of the coldest ever recorded, <u>which nobody had expected</u>.
2 When people are asked where they want to live, <u>in most cases</u> they say 'in the countryside'.
3 <u>From what I've read</u>, they're going to build a dam across the river.
4 Part of the forest was destroyed by fire, <u>which was a pity</u>.
5 A bridge collapsed during the storm. <u>It was lucky that</u> nobody was injured.
6 <u>It came as no surprise that</u> the company said it was not to blame for the oil slick.
7 Two children went missing during the flood, but <u>the good news is</u> they are now safe.
8 I don't know if there's a Recycling Centre, but <u>I'm afraid it's true</u> I haven't tried very hard to find out.
9 There's a real crisis in fishing. <u>It is clear that</u> too many boats are chasing too few fish.
10 <u>I don't know why, but</u> all the apples have disappeared from the tree in my garden.

2 Comment on each situation by writing a sentence containing a sentence adverb.

1 You have heard that summers are going to get hotter.
2 You lost your mobile phone but someone found it and gave it back to you.
3 People were asked if they wanted to give up eating meat. Most said 'no'.
4 You failed your biology exam but you know you hadn't done enough revision.
5 You hear footsteps behind you but when you look round there's no-one there.
6 A friend you haven't seen or heard from for years knocks on your door.

Part 1: essay *Page 99*

3 Discuss the questions in small groups.

1 Which picture shows each of these endangered animals?
   Black Rhinoceros   Snow leopard   Southern Water Vole   Vicuna
2 Which is native to a) Africa b) Asia c) Europe d) South America?
3 Which other creatures at risk of extinction do you know of?
4 What reasons can you think of for species becoming endangered?

4 Look at the exam task instructions and the first three notes. Answer these questions.

1 What do you have to write about, and for whom?
2 Which points must you choose from?
3 What must you also write about two of those points?

5 Look at the three opinions in the exam task. For each one, decide which of A, B or C is the best way of paraphrasing each opinion in an exam answer. Say why in each case.

1 A Protecting animals is something that people should be taught how to do.
  B Schools and the media should show the public how they can help conserve wildlife.
  C The public should be given lessons in what to do about the situation.

2 A Habitats can be restored to enable species at risk of extinction to thrive again.
  B The populations of endangered species should be encouraged to increase.
  C One way to help the recovery of endangered animal populations is to improve their environment.

3 A Laws should protect all living creatures, wherever they may be.
  B Harming animals, or damaging the places where they live, ought to be illegal.
  C There should be strict laws against the harming of wildlife or their habitats.

Exam task

> **Ways governments could help protect endangered species:**
>
> - education
> - protected zones
> - legislation

> **Some opinions expressed in the discussion:**
>
> "People should be shown how they can help conserve wildlife."
>
> "We can help endangered animal populations recover by improving their environment."
>
> "It ought to be illegal to harm animals or damage the places where they live."

Write an essay for your tutor discussing **two** of the points in your notes. You should **explain which way you think would be more effective, giving reasons** to support your opinion. You may, if you wish, make use of the opinions expressed in the discussion, but you should use your own words as far as possible.

6 Read the model essay. Then answer the questions.

1 Which two of the notes does the writer use, and in which paragraphs?
2 Which two handwritten opinions does she use, and how does she paraphrase them?
3 Which way does she think would be more effective and what reasons does she give?
4 Which of the following does she use?

- inversion of subject and verb
- sentence adverbs
- addition links
- contrast links

At no time in recorded history have so many species of animal faced extinction. Alarmingly, scientists say that our planet is currently undergoing a mass extinction episode, brought about by a combination of factors that include habitat destruction, diseases, pollution, uncontrolled hunting, and – above all – climate change.

One solution is to pass strict laws protecting both wildlife and their habitats. Not only must the hunting or capturing of endangered or threatened species be made a criminal offence, the sale, export or import of products from those animals should also be prohibited worldwide. Clearly, such regulations will be difficult to enforce in certain countries, but they are essential if the trade in ivory, for instance, is to be stopped. In addition, the law must prevent damage to natural habitats by pollution, uncontrolled building or the use of pesticides.

Another approach would be to create protected zones where a recovery plan would enable endangered animals, especially those most affected by habitat loss, to return to their previous population levels. Crucially, such zones would be kept free from water contamination, illegal hunting and invasive species, while wildlife-friendly land management practices would be encouraged and animals relocated there from less safe environments.

On balance, however, I would prefer to see legislation. Unfortunately, there simply are not the resources available to establish protected zones for all the animals at risk, and the loss of one species inevitably leads to the extinction of others within the ecosystem. The law, on the other hand, can be applied globally to combat what is now, undeniably, a global crisis.

7 You are going to do the exam task. If you intend to write about education, get ideas by thinking about these points and making notes.

- The educational system, the government and the media should make everyone aware of the threats to the survival of animal species, and the consequences of extinctions.
- People should be encouraged to help conserve wildlife by, for example, providing habitats in their gardens, avoiding the use of pesticides or not keeping invasive species as pets, and by reporting any illegal hunting, dumping of waste or water contamination.

Quick steps to writing a Part 1 essay
- If you feel strongly about the topic, use some emphatic language such as inversion of subject and object.
- Stay within the word limits. Writing too much creates a negative impression, while too little may prevent you dealing with all aspects of the task.

8 Look at the Quick steps, then plan and write your **essay** in 220–260 words in an appropriate style. When you have finished, check your work as in Unit 1, Writing Exercise 8 on page 15.

Exam tip >

As elsewhere in the exam, you can write in U.S. or U.K. English as long as you use it consistently.

Part 8

1 Explain the differences between these pairs of words.

1	a) learning	b) instruction
2	a) lecture	b) tutorial
3	a) lecturer	b) professor
4	a) scholar	b) scholarship
5	a) seminar	b) workshop
6	a) enrol	b) qualify
7	a) graduate	b) graduation
8	a) undergraduate	b) postgraduate
9	a) educated	b) educational
10	a) prospectus	b) syllabus

2 Discuss these questions.

1 What different ways of learning are shown in the pictures?
2 Which of these ways of learning do you think suits you best? Why?
3 Which other ways of learning do you like? Which do you dislike? Why?

3 Look at the exam task. Quickly read the text and decide which kind of learner is most similar to you.

Quick steps to Reading and Use of English Part 8

• When you have found an answer, read the question again and study the evidence in the text carefully.
• Cross out questions as you answer them.
• If you can't decide, eliminate the obviously incorrect letters and guess.

---

4 Look at the Quick steps, underline the key words in questions 1–10 and do the exam task.

> **Exam tip** ❭
>
> Remember that you will need to use at least one option more often than others.

Exam task

You are going to read an article in which a psychologist assesses four different kinds of learner. For questions **1–10**, choose from the kinds of learner (**A–D**). The kinds of learner may be chosen more than once.

According to the psychologist, which kind of learner …

likes to take into account what has happened in the past before they act?	1
has little interest in ensuring something remains effective once it has become operational?	2
feels the need to make sure different things fit into an overall pattern?	3
may be irritated if they encounter obstacles to the introduction of innovations?	4
quickly loses interest in conversations they believe to be pointless?	5
prefers to avoid taking part in anything that has not been sufficiently well thought through?	6
dislikes it when people fail to take the subject seriously enough?	7
enjoys participating in group activities?	8
needs to see the immediate relevance and usefulness of learning something?	9
would always be opposed to basing an opinion on insufficient evidence?	10

Four different kinds of learner

Learner A

People in this group adapt and integrate observations into complex but logically sound theories. They think problems through in a vertical, step-by-step logical way, assimilating disparate facts into coherent theories. They tend to be perfectionists who won't rest easy until everything is tidy and forms part of a rational scheme. They like to analyse and synthesise, and are keen on basic assumptions, principles, theories, models and systems. Their philosophy prizes rationality and logic, so questions they frequently ask are: 'Does it make sense?', 'How does this go with that?', and 'What are the basic assumptions?' They tend to be detached, analytical and dedicated to rational objectivity rather than anything subjective or ambiguous, approaching problems in a consistently logical manner. This is their 'mental set' and they rigidly reject anything that conflicts with it. They prefer to maximise certainty and feel uncomfortable with subjective judgements, lateral thinking and anything that treats the matter in hand with less respect than they feel it deserves.

Learner B

These people are keen on trying out ideas, theories and techniques to see if they work in practice. They positively search out new ideas and take the first opportunity to experiment with applications. They are the sort of people who return from courses brimming with new ideas that they want to try out in practice. They like to get on with things and act quickly and confidently on ideas that attract them, and are liable to resent any rules or regulations that may impede their implementation. They also tend to be impatient with discussions that they believe are not goal-orientated, and their attention soon begins to wander if they feel they are going round in circles. They are essentially practical, down to earth people who like making practical decisions and solving problems. They see problems and opportunities as a challenge, and their philosophy is: 'There is always a better way' and 'If it works, it's good'.

Learner C

People in this group involve themselves fully and without bias in new experiences, they enjoy the here and now, and are happy to be dominated by immediate experiences. They are open-minded, not sceptical, and this tends to make them enthusiastic about anything new. Their philosophy is: "I'll try anything once", so they tend to act first and consider the consequences afterwards. Their days are filled with activity and they tackle problems by brainstorming. As soon as the excitement from one activity has died down they are busy looking for the next, as they tend to thrive on the challenge of new experiences but are bored with implementation and longer term consolidation. They are gregarious people constantly involving themselves with others but, in doing so, they seek to centre all activities around themselves.

These people like to stand back to ponder experiences and observe them from many different perspectives.

Learner D

They collect data, both first hand and from others, and prefer to think about it thoroughly before coming to a conclusion. The thorough collection and analysis of data about experiences and events is what counts so they tend to postpone making definitive judgments for as long as possible. Their philosophy is to be cautious, never to make wild guesses or jump to conclusions. They are thoughtful people who like to consider all possible angles and implications before making a move, and will be reluctant to become involved in activities that others put forward without having carefully considered the likely outcome. They prefer to take a back seat in meetings and discussions, listening to others and getting the drift of the discussion before making their own points. They tend to adopt a low profile and have a slightly distant, tolerant, unruffled air about them. When they do something it is in response to earlier as well as current events, and others' observations as well as their own.

5 Use the context to explain the meanings of these expressions.

1 won't rest easy (A)
2 the matter in hand (A)
3 brimming with (B)
4 open-ended (B)
5 go round in circles (B)
6 die down (C)

7 first hand (D)
8 come to a conclusion (D)
9 what counts (D)
10 take a back seat (D)
11 getting the drift (D)
12 adopt a low profile (D)

GRAMMAR

Relative clauses *Page 94*

1 Correct the mistakes in these sentences written by exam candidates. In each case explain why it is wrong.

1 You, that have always been concerned about education, should understand this.

2 I can attend the interview any time except Friday evenings, which I have a Spanish class.

3 We were disappointed there was no price reduction for students who they were not from this country.

4 Firstly, the report on college food does not refer to its quality, what seems suspicious.

5 Seferis was a Greek poet who's work was dedicated to his country.

6 It is difficult to move to a country that you are unfamiliar with the language, culture and everything around you.

7 My job is to plan activities for club members which ages are between 16 and 18.

8 The school is advertising its Business English course which is taught very well.

9 There have been serious complaints from students, which are refusing to use the canteen.

10 In the meeting, that took place yesterday, some members made interesting suggestions.

2 Complete each sentence with a relative pronoun, adding commas if necessary. In which sentences can the relative pronoun be omitted? Why? / Why not?

1 My younger brother showed me the essay .... he had written.

2 That's the primary school .... I met my best friend.

3 On Sundays .... the library is closed I read at home.

4 Students .... parents have a low income can apply for a grant.

5 The teacher .... I liked most was Mr Anderson.

6 Maths .... was my favourite subject was our first lesson of the day.

7 My mother .... is a lecturer did her PhD at Cambridge.

8 The college .... I studied at has since closed.

3 In more formal styles, 8 above could be written *The college at which* I studied has since closed. Rewrite these sentences using a preposition + relative pronoun.

1 The research the theory is based on is unreliable.

2 The people Stephen studied with were all experts.

3 We were shown the desk the President sits at.

4 There is an Open Day that prospective students are invited to.

5 He is a philosopher who many books have been written about.

6 The day the Queen was born on was a Friday.

7 That distant star has a planet we know litttle about.

8 The person I wrote to has yet to reply.

4 We can place quantifiers such as *all of, both of* or *many of* before *which* and *whom*. Join the sentences as in the example.

Example: I read that textbook. I didn't understand half of it.
I read that textbook, half of which I didn't understand.

1 I have two sisters. They are both at university.

2 Nicky sent off two job applications. Neither of them was successful.

3 I've lost touch with most of my ex-classmates. Many of them went abroad to study.

4 This department has done a lot of research. All of it has been published.

5 Astronomers observed a large number of meteorities. Few of them reached the ground.

6 In the study we interviewed hundreds of people. The majority lived locally.

7 This is where the ancient city stood. Little of it remains today.

8 The talk was attended by a large audience. None of them left before the end.

8 READING AND USE OF ENGLISH

Words with a prefix and a suffix

1 Correct the mistakes in these sentences written by exam candidates. What is the base word in each case?

1. It is an unescapable fact that people regret things they have done.
2. The public use our firm's car park illegaly.
3. There are several reasons for the unsatisfaction of the staff.
4. Some overprotecting parents keep that role even when their kids are grown up.
5. Undeniable, there are advantages to living longer.
6. It is the children's outbringing that will help them cope with life's problems.
7. My friend unexplicably took the other boy's side.
8. Being in a winning team brings an undescribable feeling of pride.

Spelling changes

2 The words in the box form new words by changing their internal spelling. Make these changes and complete the sentences.

> broad   depth   detain   maintain   prove
> repeat   resolve   strong

1. The police now have sufficient .... that the men stole the computers.
2. The river is being .... to allow bigger ships to reach the port.
3. Our aim is to .... the cultural ties between the two countries.
4. The old college building needs a lot of expensive ....
5. For somebody so young, Mia has an amazing .... of knowledge.
6. Urgent talks are taking place to find a .... to the crisis.
7. Try to avoid any .... of those mistakes.
8. At my parents' school, ... was a common punishment.

Part 3

> **Quick steps to Reading and Use of English Part 3**
> • Remember that answers may depend on the whole context, not just the words before and after the gap.
> • Check whether the word in capitals needs more than one change.

3 Quickly read the text and answer the questions.

1. What are 'employability skills'?
2. Do you think they are a useful addition to university courses?

4 Do the exam task. Which answers require both a prefix and a suffix? Which need internal spelling changes?

> **Exam tip ❯**
>
> If you need a noun, decide if it is countable or uncountable.

Exam task

For questions **1–8**, read the text below. Use the word given in capitals at the end of some of the lines to form a word that fits in the gap **in the same line**. There is an example at the beginning (**0**).

Example: **0** REASONABLY

Graduates need employability skills

Years ago, anyone with a degree could be **(0)** .... confident of finding a job.	**REASON**
But with ever more graduates looking for work, that confidence has now been replaced by **(1)** .... even among those with a Master's. Graduates,	**CERTAIN**
no matter how well qualified, are **(2)** .... being required to show they also have 'employability	**INCREASE**
skills', such as numeracy, business awareness and the **(3)** .... to deal with problems creatively.	**CAPABLE**
Fortunately for **(4)** .... undergraduates, many	**PROSPECT**
universities already aim to develop such skills as part of their courses, frequently with the help of professional **(5)** .... working in the relevant	**ADVICE**
business sector. The approach often has both **(6)** .... and practical elements, for instance	**THEORY**
designing a marketing campaign and then working with actual clients.	
Activities are done in groups, thus **(7)** .... that	**SURE**
students become used to team work. Any **(8)**	**WILLING**
to take part can be overcome by pointing out that for many employers the ability to work in a team is essential.	

Part 2

1 Work in small groups. Which of the expressions in the box mean a–e? What differences in meaning are there?

> appoint   be employed   dismiss
> fill a position   fire   go into   hire
> hold down a job   lay off   let go
> make redundant   on benefits   out of a job
> practise   quit   recruit   resign   retire
> sack   serve   step down   take on

a) get or do a job
b) give somebody a job
c) leave a job
d) make somebody leave a job
e) without a job

2 Discuss these questions.

1 How many people are out of work in your country?
2 In which industries have a lot of people been laid off?
3 What are the most common reasons for people being dismissed?
4 Why do some people find it difficult to hold down a job?
5 Which organisations recruit people of your age?
6 What kind of work or profession would you like to go into?
7 What would make you resign from a job?
8 At what age would you like to retire?

3 Look at the photo and answer the questions about being an airline pilot.

1 What personal qualities are needed?
2 What training is required?
3 What are the advantages and disadvantages of the work?

Quick steps to Listening Part 2

- Be sure you know how numbers, including ordinals (1st, 2nd, etc.) and fractions, are pronounced.
- Take care with words or numbers that appear to fit a gap, but are not the right answer.
- Write up to three words.

4 Study the exam task. What kind of word, phrase or number is needed for each answer?

5 🔘 **2.09** Read the Quick steps and Exam tip, then do the exam task.

Exam task

You will hear airline pilot Anita Ricci talking about her work. For questions **1–8**, complete the sentences with a word or short phrase.

> ### My job: airline pilot
>
> Anita's **(1)** .... wasn't good enough for her to become a military pilot.
>
> Most airline pilots start their careers as a **(2)** .... pilot.
>
> It is becoming less common to have a **(3)** .... on an aeroplane.
>
> Anita cannot fly a plane on her present route for more than **(4)** .... without a break.
>
> Anita likes flying into Swiss airports because of the excellent **(5)** .... there.
>
> Anita says that as a pilot you have to be able to accept **(6)** .... from others.
>
> Over **(7)** .... pilots applied recently to work for Anita's company.
>
> Anita says airlines are particularly sensitive to changes in **(8)** ....

Exam tip ▸

It is simpler to write any numbers as figures, for example *96* rather than *ninety-six*. You also avoid the risk of making spelling mistakes.

8 SPEAKING

Adding emphasis

1 For each of a–d, complete the second sentence with one word. Then answer questions 1–4 about each of those sentences.

a) I want to study physics at university.
   What I want to study at university … physics.

b) I took the job as I needed the money.
   The reason I took the job … that I needed the money.

c) The manager replied to my email.
   The person who replied to my email … the manager.

d) I sent off my application last month.
   It …. last month when I sent off my application.

1 Which information is emphasised?
2 How does the sentence begin?
3 What comes before a form of the verb *be*?
4 Is any other change needed?

2 Rewrite the sentences to emphasise the underlined expressions, using the words in brackets.

1 You need to <u>work harder</u>. (What)
2 <u>Travelling to work</u> causes the most stress. (It)
3 <u>Bankers</u> seem to make the most money. (The people)
4 Emma resigned because <u>she didn't like her boss</u>. (The reason)
5 I found <u>all the form-filling</u> really boring. (It)
6 My friend and I first met at <u>the office</u>. (The place)

3 Tell your partner the following, using emphatic forms from Exercises 1 and 2.

1 The job you'd most like to do.
2 The most boring thing you have to do.
3 The country you'd most like to live in.
4 The kind of people who annoy you most.
5 The time when you feel most relaxed.
6 Something you would like to achieve.

Part 4   *Page 111*

> **Quick steps to Speaking Part 4**
> • Whenever the examiner asks you a question, try to think of two or three replies.
> • If you prefer not to give an opinion immediately, say something like *It depends* or *I'm not sure*, and outline arguments on both sides.
> • If you partly agree with an opinion, say something like *Yes, up to a point, but …*

4 🎧 **2.10** Listen to this extract from Maxim and Dariya practising Part 4 and answer the questions.

1 What question does the teacher ask them?
2 Which speaker considers arguments on both sides before giving their opinion?
3 Does the other speaker completely agree?

5 🎧 **2.10** Listen again and answer the questions.

1 What expressions does Maxim use to avoid giving an opinion immediately?
2 What expression does Dariya use to show she partly agrees with Maxim?
3 Which phrases beginning *What …* and *It …* do they use?

6 In groups of three, do Part 4 three times. Each time, one of you is the examiner. Follow these instructions.

1 Ask the 'candidates' three questions, if necessary prompting with *Why?* or *Do you agree?*
2 Stop them after five minutes and comment on how well they did the task.

List of questions for Speaking Part 4

1 Which jobs in your country are considered to be good jobs?
2 Which job would you least like to do?
3 Would you prefer to work on your own or as part of a working team?
4 Do you think it is more important to make a lot of money or to enjoy your job?
5 In what ways do you think people's working conditions should be improved?
6 Why do some people find it difficult to choose a career?
7 Would you prefer to have one career, or a series of different jobs during your working life?
8 Which is more important for an employee: qualifications or experience?
9 Which is better: working in an office or working online from home?

> **Exam tip ›**
>
> Don't worry if the examiner stops you before you have said everything you intended to. There is a strict time limit for each part of the Speaking test.

Formal language

1 Which of these are common in formal writing, and which are more likely to be found in informal writing?

1	long words	6	conversation expressions
2	exclamation marks	7	contracted forms of words
3	passive forms	8	impersonal tone
4	long, complete sentences	9	question tags
5	phrasal verbs	10	abbreviations

2 Replace the <u>underlined</u> informal expressions with more formal words from the box.

> are well informed   understand the situation   excessive
> extremely disappointed   fortunate   misunderstand me
> I am quite interested in   I was completely unaware

1 <u>I like the sound of</u> the vacancy advertised by your company.
2 I feel the price you have quoted me is <u>over the top</u>.
3 Please don't <u>get me wrong</u> when I make this point.
4 I realise that I am <u>in luck</u> to be given this opportunity.
5 <u>It's news to me</u> that the firm intends to close this office.
6 I would be <u>gutted</u> not to be offered this position.
7 I am extremely grateful for your explanation. I now completely <u>get the picture</u>.
8 It is clear from our correspondence that you <u>know your stuff</u>.

Part 2: formal letter *Page 101*

3 'Work experience' typically involves school or college students doing one or two weeks unpaid work in term time. Discuss these questions in small groups.

1 What are the advantages for students of doing work experience?
2 How does the employer also benefit?
3 If you are a student, what kind of work experience would you like to do? If you are already working, what kind would you like to have done when you were at school?

4 Look at the exam task and answer the questions.

1 Who are you writing to?
2 Why are you writing to them?
3 What must your letter contain?
4 What style should you write in?

Exam task

> Your company has a number of vacancies for students who wish to do two weeks' work experience during the next summer term. You have been asked by your manager to write a letter to a local college. Your letter should explain:
>
> - what your company does
> - what kind of work the students would do
> - how they would benefit from working for the company.
>
> Write your letter.

5 Which of the following would be appropriate for this task? Which would not? Why?

1 They can chill out with their mates in the coffee bar.
2 They would develop their skills in a professional working environment.
3 We've got loads of fun jobs for the guys at your college.
4 The full-time staff would ensure they made the most of their time here.
5 Check out our website for more info!
6 I trust you will find this information helpful.
7 I look forward to hearing from you.
8 Speak soon.

6 Quickly read the model letter below. In which paragraph does the writer do each of the following?

1 describe the work students would do
2 say what her company does
3 outline its work experience programme
4 suggest what the reader should now do
5 give a reason for writing
6 explain how students would benefit

Dear Sir or Madam,

I am writing to inform you that this hotel will be able to offer work experience to twelve students aged 16 to 18 during the summer term. Placements will last a fortnight and no wages will be paid.

The hotel employs over 100 full-time staff, the majority of whom live in the local community. In addition to providing luxury accommodation, we serve high quality meals in our restaurant and café, and offer extensive leisure facilities including a gymnasium, swimming pool and sauna.

Placements will involve working with reception staff, housekeepers, maintenance workers and porters, kitchen staff and waiters, fitness instructors and lifeguards. Young people will be expected to carry out the same tasks as permanent employees, but suitable training will be given. They will receive health and safety instruction when their placement commences, and will be supervised at all times. They will also be assessed throughout and receive constructive advice from their supervisors.

On successful completion of their placement, students will be awarded a Work Experience Certificate and a detailed description of the work they have done, both of which will be useful additions to their CV. Moreover, their placement will introduce them to the world of work, possibly giving them ideas for careers and enabling them to make contacts for future networking. What will benefit them most, however, is the opportunity to develop their employability skills, regarded by many employers as essential for those seeking their first job.

I would be most grateful if you could pass this information on to your students.

Yours faithfully,
Montserrat Oriol

---

7 Answer the questions about the model letter.

1 In what style is the letter written?
2 What formal beginning and ending does the writer use?
3 Which two quantifier + preposition + relative pronoun forms does she use?
4 Which emphatic *What* form does she use?
5 Which formal expressions in the letter mean the following?

tell	big	gym	staff	training	begins	looking for	very pleased

8 Read these exam task instructions and answer the questions in Exercise 4 about it.

Exam task

You see this newspaper advertisement.

The Central has vacancies for young people on our annual two-week Work Experience programme. Unpaid work will be available in our kitchens, restaurants and leisure facilities, as well as in maintenance, housekeeping and reception.

Tell us which job you would like to do and why, why you would be suited to working in a hotel environment, and what you hope to learn from the experience.

Send your application to: Ms Klaudia Nowak, Human Resources Manager, Central Hotel

Write your **letter**.

9 Look at the Quick steps and plan your letter. Which of these points are relevant to this exam task?

1 your willingness to learn from others
2 your experiences as a hotel guest
3 what you want to find out about yourself
4 how much you would like to earn
5 any experience you already have of the work you want to do
6 why you should be given a management position at the hotel
7 how you rate your interpersonal skills
8 your capacity to work hard

10 Write your **letter** in **220–260** words in an appropriate style. When you have finished, check your work as in Unit 1, Writing Exercise 8 on page 15.

Exam tip ›

Don't include any postal email addresses in the Writing paper.

9 Science and technology
LISTENING

Science vocabulary

1 Work in small groups. Make sure you understand these words, then discuss the questions.

> analysis   approach   concept   criteria
> deduction   evaluation   factors   features
> hypothesis   method   principle   procedure
> relevance   significance   theory   variables

1 Which picture shows the way you are or were usually taught science? Which do you think is more effective?
2 Which is or was your favourite science subject at school? Which did you like least?
3 Which was the most interesting scientific experiment you have ever done?
4 What would you like to use science to find out? How would you do it?

Part 3

2 Discuss these questions.

1 What do you think happens at a science fair (a competitive exhibition of science projects) for young people, and how do students prepare for it?
2 Have you ever taken part in one? If not, would you like to? Why? / Why not?

> **Quick steps to Listening Part 3**
> • Read the questions in the pause after the instructions.
> • Decide what kind of information, e.g. a regret, is needed.
> • The first time you listen, don't worry if you miss a question. Leave it and go on to the next one.
> • On the second listening, answer questions you missed.

Exam task

🔘 **2.11** You will hear an interview with physics teacher Kieran Shaw, who has taken his students to a Science Fair. For questions **1–6**, choose the answer (**A, B, C** or **D**) which fits best according to what you hear.

1 What does Kieran criticise about the previous Science Fair?
A the number of prizes
B the standard of judging
C the quality of the projects
D the number of projects

2 Kieran says the fall in the number of participants at some science fairs might be caused by
A a belief that science fairs are old-fashioned.
B worry among parents about the cost of projects.
C reluctance to attend science fairs at weekends.
D a general reduction in schools' budgets.

3 Which does Kieran believe is a problem among his students?
A parents giving students too much help
B more boys than girls involved in projects
C rich students having more resources for projects
D too much emphasis on competition rather than cooperation

4 Kieran says the most important factor in choosing a topic is whether it is likely to
A need expensive equipment in order to do experiments.
B keep the students interested throughout the project.
C be sufficiently simple for students of that age group.
D differ significantly from the topics chosen by others.

5 According to Kieran, what mistake do some students make during their presentation?
A They don't go into enough detail about their project.
B They can't remember the speech they memorised.
C They tend to speak too slowly to the judges.
D They use words they don't fully understand.

6 Kieran predicts that this year's winner will be the project about
A the variation in people's eyesight during the day.
B the relative cleanliness of different objects.
C the coolest clothes to wear in summer.
D the best place to store fruit.

Exam tip ❯

Remember that the questions follow the order of the information in the recording.

9 GRAMMAR

Modal verbs  G Page 96

1 ⊙ Correct the mistakes in these sentences written by exam candidates. Explain why each sentence is wrong.

1 In the end I could solve the problem by paying cash.
2 Suddenly the lights went out and I must find my way out in the dark.
3 In this catalogue there is a printer that can interest us.
4 You mustn't bring much money because you'll be staying at my house.
5 You've been overworking so you can have developed some health problems.
6 It had to be very hard to survive in prehistoric times with those dangerous animals around.
7 Yesterday's accident can be prevented.
8 They left the refrigerator full of food so we needn't go to the supermarket when we arrived.

2 Choose the correct option and say why it is right.

1 Free samples of this product *must / can / need to* be obtained by going to our website.
2 Jeremy copied his biology essay from the Internet. He *may not / shouldn't / mustn't* have done that.
3 In those days, dangerous chemicals *could / may / were able to* be bought in the shops.
4 I heard your company is closing down. You *have to / should / must* be very worried.
5 Students *shouldn't / mustn't / needn't* pay to go into the Science Museum.
6 You *can / might / must* have burnt your hands if you hadn't been wearing gloves.
7 That group only started their project last week. They *mustn't / mightn't / can't* have finished already!
8 The lab has been completely destroyed. There *might / must / should* have been a huge explosion.
9 If you're not feeling well, Annie, I think you *should / must / have to* stay at home today.
10 You *didn't need to take / needn't have taken / didn't have to take* a taxi. I could have picked you up from the station.

3 Reply to the comments by using a form of the modal in brackets.

Example: I think I saw you downtown last night. (could)
You couldn't have done. I was at home all the time.

1 This crowd is huge. I wonder how many people are here? (must)
2 I've got no money at all left. (should)
3 It was compulsory at my school to do double maths from the age of 14. (have to)
4 I left my phone on the bar and now it's gone! (must)
5 Marcos and Anna set off in the car six hours ago, but they still haven't arrived. (might)

6 The chemistry exam was so difficult, wasn't it? (be able to)
7 Mr Grey always carries his umbrella. He even took it with him to Dubai! (need)
8 I'm sure I've just seen a family of aliens! (can)

4 Complete the second sentence so that it has a similar meaning to the first sentence, using the word given. Do not change the word given. You must use between three and six words, including the word given.

1 I think it was a mistake to send that email to her.
   SHOULD
   I don't think .... that email.

2 I regret not being able to complete my project on time.
   COMPLETED
   I wish .... my project on time.

3 It would be fairer to candidates if making a speech were voluntary.
   HAVE
   It would be fairer if candidates .... a speech.

4 It's possible that I broke the glass by accident, though I didn't notice doing so.
   MIGHT
   I .... the glass, though I didn't notice doing so.

5 It was wrong to let people take part in such a dangerous experiment.
   ALLOWED
   People .... take part in such a dangerous experiment.

6 Carmela said that she was going to call me, but it looks like she's forgotten.
   MUST
   Carmela .... that she would call me.

Exam task

You are going to read a newspaper article about science on television. For questions **1–6**, choose the answer (**A**, **B**, **C** or **D**) which you think fits best according to the text.

Science on TV: it's not dumb, but it could be smarter

Science broadcasting would be greatly improved by involving viewers in the experimental process, says Alice Bell

A new science series started on television last month. Cue lots of people muttering about dumbing down, casting disapproving looks in the presenting scientist's direction. They shouldn't. Complaining about dumbing down is dumb. It misses what all good popularisation does. It also detracts from other questions about science programmes. Is there too much focus on what scientific thought delivers, not the methods, processes and politics that make it? Does television too often package science as a pantomime set of characters rather than connect the public to the reality of research? Is it stuck in the past?   line

Science changes as it makes its way on to television, just as it does as it travels to newspapers, magazines, books, exams and through the various media of the scientific community (journals, emails, gossip over coffee at a conference). People who take a dim view of media professors need to get over themselves and stop assuming the difference between professional and popular science sits on a hierarchical frame that places the former on top. Popularisation doesn't make knowledge something less than it was. Often it picks up new perspectives as well as simply inviting more people to support or even be part of the enterprise. Done well, popularisation isn't pathological to research; it's lifeblood.

Still, there are problems with many traditional approaches to the way we share science. There is a history of snobbishness against scientists who take time to talk to the public, but equally silly is a snobbishness against presenters who aren't actually scientists. These days the more

1 Discuss the questions.

1 Compare the pictures. What impression of science and scientists does each give? Which do you think is closer to the reality of working in science?
2 What are TV science programmes like in your country? How could they be improved?

2 Quickly read the exam text and answer these questions.

1 What are the meanings of a) *dumb* in the title and b) *dumbing down* in the first paragraph?
2 What does the introduction tell you about the purpose of the text?
3 In what ways are the writer's views similar or different to your answers to question 2 in Exercise 1?

Quick steps to Reading and Use of English Part 5

- For items like *The word 'this' in line 5 refers to …*, study the sentences immediately before and after it.
- If an item says the writer aims *to show* something, look for an example.
- Where an item says the writer *implies* something, look for what they indicate about it without saying so directly.
- Don't leave any blanks, make an intelligent guess.

3 Study the Quick steps, then look at the beginning of each question. Which focus on:

a) the writer's opinion or attitude?
b) a suggestion by the writer?
c) an example?
d) a reference word?

4 Do the exam task.

Exam tip ›

Choose your answers by focusing on what the text says, not on your own knowledge of or opinions about the topic.

serious TV channels favour professional scientists to present, even if they rarely write the script and often stray outside their area of expertise. It's a shallow form of scientific authenticity, and one that patronises the audience and curtails scientific expertise.

I especially worry that science is often rendered as something to be simply consumed by the public. If we're using the metaphor of scientific literacy, in a sense it's 'read-only' research. Retelling science for explanatory or entertainment purposes might give us a great picture of what the scientific idea looks like, but often removes a lot about how the scientists got to these conclusions. It doesn't show the workings of science or share the science-in-the-making, meaning it's harder to critique or get involved with – or simply enjoy as entertaining and educational in itself. I'd like to see an attempt to share the means of production of science, not just sell its products.

The interviews with working scientists on a current radio series bring out the texture of science, a sense of what drives scientists, the frustrations, boredom, adventure and accidents their work can include. But this is still a matter of telling a story rather than involving audiences. That's not to say I'm against storytelling science, just that we have to be aware of the narrative forces in play. Some time ago there was a lot of fuss about a nature documentary filming polar bear cubs in a wildlife centre rather than in the wild, as appeared to be the case. But this sort of fabrication is routine, just as we routinely leave out bits of science to tell interesting, exciting and useful stories. We'd get lost otherwise. Televisual science is always a construction, and it's often worth deconstructing and arguing over how we choose to do this. But it can be a meaningful and necessary construction too, just as a scientific paper is a meaningful construction we might argue over.

I don't mind the odd bit of sparkle and showmanship around science. Nor do I mind shows that just invite audiences to passively watch or listen – as long as we have more critical and interactive projects too. We might be in a golden age of science television but we shouldn't stop asking questions about it. We need to be imaginative about what science is, who it talks to and how it might be better; not simply find ever more ways to spread the status quo.

1 The word 'it' in line 13 refers to
   A the current approach to research in science.
   B the way the broadcast media cover science.
   C the attitude of politicians towards science.
   D how the public see science and scientists.

2 What point is the writer making in the second paragraph?
   A Science can benefit from becoming more popular.
   B Popular science is inferior to professional science.
   C Scientific journals report on science without altering it.
   D The quality of research is being harmed by popular science.

3 What is the writer's attitude to the presenting of science programmes?
   A Science programmes should always be presented by actual scientists.
   B Presenters often seem to assume that viewers know nothing about science.
   C Television scientists should talk only about their own branch of science.
   D Scientists should be working in science, not presenting TV shows.

4 The writer believes that the public are frequently being denied
   A the opportunity to enjoy programmes about science.
   B information about the results of scientific research.
   C the experience of hearing scientists talk about their work.
   D an insight into how the scientific process works.

5 The writer mentions the programme about polar bears to show that
   A scientists often find it impossible to agree with one another.
   B the makers of science documentaries are often untrustworthy.
   C in science it is impossible to report every detail of the story.
   D documentaries cannot show the scientific process realistically.

6 What does the writer call for in the last paragraph?
   A an end to the trivialisation of science in television programmes
   B a more balanced approach when covering science on television
   C greater public awareness of the current nature of science
   D television quiz shows that focus exclusively on science

5 Find expressions in the text with these meanings (paragraph numbers in brackets).

1 this is the signal for (something to begin) (1)
2 show disapproval (2)
3 the first of two (previously mentioned things or people) (2)
4 considered in a particular way (4)
5 involves (5)
6 that are having an effect (5)
7 an occasional (6)
8 existing situation (6)

Part 2

Dependent prepositions

1 Look at these extracts from the Reading text on page 75.

We have to be <u>aware of</u> the narrative forces ...

We need to be <u>imaginative about</u> what science is ...

Which preposition, *about, against, by, for, in, of, to,* or *with*, often follows each of the C1-level adjectives in the box?

> alert   biased   compatible   deprived   eligible   equivalent   frustrated   hostile   inadequate   insensitive   knowledgeable   notorious   prejudiced   protective   resident   restricted   superior   untouched

2 👁 Which of these sentences written by exam candidates contain an incorrect preposition? Correct any errors.

1 The village is adjacent by the sea.
2 That information is not consistent with the truth.
3 A smart phone would be very handy to reading my e-mails.
4 Some people are ignorant of the basic principles of science.
5 The ideal candidate has to be receptive of new ideas.
6 Japan is renowned for its innovations in technology.
7 Alfonso, horrified of what he had seen, called the police.
8 At first, Elena was sceptical to what the archaeologist was telling her.

3 Complete the sentences with the adjectives in the box plus suitable prepositions.

> eligible   equivalent   handy   ignorant   notorious   renowned   restricted   sceptical

1 To avoid overcrowding, the number of visitors was .... six hundred.
2 This little device is .... measuring height and distance.
3 One mile is .... about 1.6 kilometres.
4 The research was flawed so we are .... the results.
5 You have to be aged 18 or over to be .... this competition.
6 That man is either .... the facts, or simply not telling the truth.
7 It's a particularly dangerous road, ... serious accidents.
8 Cambridge University is .... academic excellence in teaching and research.

> **Quick steps to Reading and Use of English Part 2**
> • Remember that every gap must be filled in.
> • Pencil in your answers on the question paper so you can easily check the completed text makes sense.
> • Never write two answers.
> • Check your spelling.

4 Read the text quickly. How does the writer answer the question in the title?

5 The example answer completes the expression *distracted by*. As you do the exam task, decide which prepositions can go with the words next to gaps 2, 4, 5 and 7.

> **Exam tip** ❯
> Use capital letters when you write on the answer sheet.

Exam task

For questions **1–8**, read the text below and think of the word that best fits each gap. Use only **one** word in each gap. There is an example at the beginning (**0**).

Example: 0 BY

> ### Why are overheard calls so annoying?
>
> People are more distracted **(0)** .... mobile phone conversations than background chat in the same room, **(1)** .... to a study at San Diego University.
>
> The research also shows that an overheard phone conversation is significantly more memorable **(2)** .... someone involuntarily listening in than if the conversation **(3)** .... place between people in the same location.
>
> Volunteers were asked to do anagram puzzles while, unknown **(4)** .... them, researchers conducted a scripted conversation in the background, either between two people in the room or between someone on a mobile phone and an unknown caller.
>
> Participants only heard the conversation once and were unaware **(5)** .... the fact it was part of the study. Those **(6)** .... overheard the one-sided conversation found it more distracting and annoying, and remembered more words from it.
>
> A possible explanation is that we keep trying to figure out what is going on, becoming frustrated **(7)** .... our failure to do so. **(8)** .... knowing where the conversation is heading is what makes overheard cell-phone calls so irritating.

9 SPEAKING

Speaking

1 🔊 **2.12** Use modal verbs to complete this conversation between two bus passengers. Then listen to check your answers.

A: 'Hey, that's a long queue!'
B: 'Some of them are looking fed up. They (1) .... standing there for hours.'
A: 'Yes, they (2) .... been. I wonder why?'
B: 'They (3) .... hoping to get tickets for that concert.'
A: 'I suppose they (4) .... be. Or they (5) .... queuing for the sales. They start later today.'

2 In pairs, use modals with *-ing* to speculate about these situations.

Example: You see two people looking angry with each other.
They might have been arguing. OR They must be getting on badly.

1 It's nearly exam time and your classmate is looking very tired.
2 There's a big football match on but you don't know how your team is doing.
3 You're phoning a friend who's on a train, but you lose the connection.
4 You get up in the morning and see there's half a metre of snow outside.
5 You call round at friend's house on a Saturday morning but there's no-one in.
6 You wake up in the middle of the night thinking you've just won the lottery.

Part 2 🅢 *Page 108*

3 🔊 **2.13** Read the exam task instructions. Then listen to two strong students, Nico and Mia, talking about two of these pictures and answer these questions.

1 Which photos does Nico compare?
2 How does he say those jobs were done in the past?
3 What difficulties nowadays does he mention?
4 Which technological advance does Mia choose? Why?

4 🔊 **2.13** Listen again. Which of these do Nico and Mia use to speculate about the pictures?

a) modal + *be* + *-ing*
b) modal + *have* + past participle

Quick steps to Speaking Part 2
- Use modal forms + *ing* to speculate about present and recent events.
- If you make a mistake, you can correct it, but don't keep stopping or you won't have time to complete the task.
- Talk until the examiner stops you.

Exam task

Each of you will be given three pictures. You have to talk about **two** of them on your own for about a minute, and also to answer a question briefly about your partner's pictures.

Candidate A, it's your turn first. Here are your pictures. They show people **working with different kinds of technology**. Compare **two** of the pictures, and say **how the jobs might have been done in the past, and how difficult it might be for the people to work with this technology.**

Candidate B, **which of these technological advances do you think is the most beneficial to society?**

> How might the jobs have been done in the past?
> How difficult might it be for the people to work with this technology?

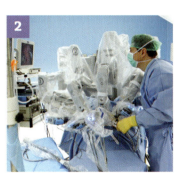

5 Work in groups of three and do the exam task using pictures 1 and 2. Then change roles and do the task twice more, using pictures 2 and 3 and then pictures 1 and 3.

6 Tell the others in your group how well you think they did Part 2, and listen to their comments on your speaking.

Exam tip 〉

Practise for the exam by timing yourself speaking for 60 seconds.

9 WRITING

Result links

1 Complete the sentences with the words in the box. Which are formal? Which form fixed phrases? Underline these, as in the example.

account   consequence   consequently   else   otherwise
owing   reason   result   so   such   view

Example: Sales of the device have fallen <u>as a *result* of</u> price rises.

1 There is less rainfall nowadays and for that .... the desert is growing.
2 Robots are now .... sophisticated that they can carry out many household tasks.
3 Some people prefer not to use credit cards online .... to the risk of theft.
4 More tests must be done on this new medicine. .... , people's health could be at risk.
5 The new device was found to be unsafe and in .... production was ended.
6 On .... of the high radiation levels, long-distance space travel may be impossible.
7 It's .... a great invention that I don't know how I managed without it!
8 We must build higher sea defences or .... the city will one day be flooded.
9 More and more people are shopping online. .... , some stores have gone out of business.
10 In .... of the fact that people can watch TV online, television sets may become obsolete.

2 Rewrite the sentences using the words in brackets.

1 The project was abandoned as it had gone over budget. (consequence)
2 The instructions were too complicated for me to understand. (so)
3 There was a defect in the device so it was withdrawn from sale. (account)
4 If you don't charge your phone up soon, the battery will run out. (else)
5 A virus got into the system, leading to all the computers crashing. (consequently)
6 I can't stop playing that game because it's so addictive. (such)
7 The temperature suddenly rose so the machine stopped working. (owing)
8 If I kept looking at my email, I'd spend all day answering messages. (otherwise)

Part 2: report   *Page 103*

3 Look at the pictures and answer the questions.

1 What do you think these astronomers enjoy about their work?
2 Which other jobs in science do you think would be interesting and/or rewarding?
3 Have you ever considered a career in science? Why? / Why not?

4 Answer the questions about this exam task.

1 What is the topic of the report?
2 Who are you writing for and why do they want a report?
3 What points must you include?

Exam task

Your school wants to increase the percentage of its students studying science subjects to advanced level. The head teacher has asked you to write a report on attitudes towards science among the students.

Your report should evaluate the appeal of science at the school, explain why comparatively few students want to become scientists, and suggest ways of encouraging more of them to consider a future career in science.

Write your **report**.

5 Quickly read the model report on page 79 and write a brief heading above each paragraph.

Science at school and at work

A ....

Concern has been expressed about a relative lack of interest in science as a school subject or future career. This report focuses on the views of students and puts forward suggestions for improving the image of science.

B ....

The vast majority of students who opt for science subjects feel they made the right decision. They enjoy conducting experiments in the well-equipped laboratories and appreciate the fact that the teaching staff are more highly qualified than their counterparts in arts subjects. In consequence, science students believe they are learning in a more stimulating environment.

C ....

Unfortunately, however, some students think twice before choosing sciences, owing to their reputation as comparatively difficult subjects that involve memorising facts and figures. Moreover, there is a widespread belief that high marks are harder to obtain in the sciences.

D ....

In addition, science has a serious image problem. Many are discouraged by the perceived lack of glamour of science as a profession, by film stereotypes of mad professors and computer geeks, and by the suspicion with which the media often treat scientific research, for instance concerning genetically modified food.

E ....

To create a more positive impression of science, students should be invited to participate in Science Fair projects, scientific work experience programmes and virtual Open Days at university science faculties. They should also be made aware of the benefits of studying science, such as developing thinking skills, discovering how things work and – one day – finding real solutions to real problems.

6 Read the model report again and answer the questions.

1 Which paragraph deals with each of the points in the exam task instructions?
2 How does the writer introduce the topic of the report?
3 What style is the report written in? Give some examples.
4 Which result links are used in paragraphs B and C?
5 What four suggestions are there in the final paragraph? Do you agree with them?

7 Look at these exam task instructions and answer the questions in Exercise 4 about it.

Exam task

Your job involves making long-distance business trips. Colleagues who are about to begin making similar trips have asked you which electronic device you always take with you when you travel. Now they have requested a report on that device.

Your report should explain why you chose that kind of device, evaluate its usefulness in practice, and suggest how it could be improved.

Write your **report.**

8 In pairs, think of three kinds of portable electronic device and discuss these questions about each.

1 How convenient is it to carry?
2 How easy is it to use?
3 What drawbacks or limitations does it have?
4 How could these problems be overcome?

9 Choose one of the types of device you discussed in Exercise 8. Then look at the Quick steps and plan your report.

Quick steps to writing a Part 2 report
- Underline the key words as you read the instructions.
- Think about who you are writing for and what they will want to know.
- Use your own words, not those in the instructions.
- Use a variety of structures and vocabulary.
- Check that any headings reflect the content of the paragraphs.

10 Write your **report** in 220–260 words in an appropriate style. When you have finished, check your work as in Unit 1, Writing Exercise 8 on page 15.

Exam tip >

If you don't know enough facts about the topic to write a report on it, choose another question.

10 A mind of one's own
READING AND USE OF ENGLISH

1 Complete the definitions with the words *extrovert* and *introvert*, then answer the questions.

  1 a) An .... is very confident and likes being with other people.

  b) An .... is shy, quiet and often prefers to be alone.

  2 Which photo shows someone with each of these traits?

  3 In what other ways might they differ from each other?

2 How extrovert or introvert are you? Do this quiz!

Extrovert/Introvert Quiz	Yes	No
1 I prefer one-to-one conversations to group activities.	☐	☐
2 I often prefer to express myself in writing.	☐	☐
3 I seem to care less than my peers about wealth, fame and status.	☐	☐
4 I dislike small talk, but I enjoy talking in depth about topics that matter to me.	☐	☐
5 People tell me that I'm a good listener.	☐	☐
6 People say I talk quietly.	☐	☐
7 I prefer not to show or discuss my work with others until it's finished.	☐	☐
8 I do my best work on my own.	☐	☐
9 I tend to think before I speak.	☐	☐
10 I often let calls go through to voicemail.	☐	☐
11 I can concentrate easily.	☐	☐
12 In classroom situations, I prefer lectures to seminars.	☐	☐

3 Check the meanings of the words in the box used in academic writing. Use them to complete the sentences.

> proposition   perception   questionable   classification   merit   consistently

  1 This basic diagram shows the .... of animals into two main groups.

  2 In your essay, discuss the main points for and against the following ....

  3 The research has been of a .... high standard and thoroughly deserves the prize.

  4 It is .... whether this new treatment can actually reduce stress.

  5 The draft plans for reforming local health care have .... and should be given serious consideration.

  6 Our .... of what constitutes 'normal' behaviour has changed in recent decades.

Quick steps to Reading and Use of English Part 6

• Where an item relates to all four extracts, draw a vertical line next to the relevant part of each.

• Remember not all parts of the text are tested.

• If you're unsure of any answers, eliminate any that are clearly wrong and then guess.

4 Quickly read the text. Which of the reviews is/are:

  • generally positive?

  • generally negative?

  • partly positive and partly negative?

5 Answer these questions about the exam task.

  1 What are the key words or phrases in each item?

  2 Which item involves finding information in all four reviews?

6 Do the exam task, remembering to mark the relevant parts of each review.

Exam tip

Remember that you may not need to understand every word in the text to answer the questions.

Exam task

You are going to read four reviews of a book about different personality types. For questions **1–4**, choose from the reviews **A–D**. The reviews may be chosen more than once.

Which reviewer

makes a similar criticism of Cain's apparent lack of objectivity as reviewer B?	1
disagrees with reviewer C about the strength of Cain's main argument?	2
expresses a different view from the others regarding Cain's division of people into two categories?	3
has a different view to reviewer D about who will enjoy this book?	4

Quiet
Four reviewers comment on Susan Cain's book Quiet: The Power of Introverts in a World That Can't Stop Talking

A Cain's central proposition is that over the past century the US has moved from a 'culture of character' to a 'culture of personality', as social admiration has shifted from ideals of private honour to public perception, leading to the inexorable rise of the 'extrovert ideal'. I find this highly questionable, and Cain also appears to be setting up a new categorisation which does not hold water. Extrovert and introvert are simply not the same sort of things as female/male, black/white or alive/dead; it is more useful to see the terms as adjectives, describing points on a long, loose arc than as identities. Overall, this is a remarkably noisy 'extroverted' book, bombarding the reader with unharmonious 'facts' and psychobabble ('over stimulating', to use one of Cain's terms). Lovers of quiet won't like Quiet – we would rather go for a nice walk in the country.

B Quiet is written for introverts. This involves telling us how great introverts are, how they are so sensitive you can measure their responses to things by how much their pupils dilate when faced with loud music or flashing lights. They think harder about things before they do them, and spend fruitful hours alone. At some points in this book, it is hard to avoid the impression that extroverts are bullies or at least that Cain's simplistic extrovert/introvert contrast is really a balance of jock versus geek, played out so reliably in movies about US high schools. Cain does everything she can to play this down, and say that extroverts can read this book, too (she has sales to consider, after all); but in test after test, outgoing individuals respond less well to difficult upbringings, cope less well when deprived of sleep, and are missing out on the evolutionary advantages of blushing.

C This book has a convincing idea at its heart: that the western world has become so enamoured of what Susan Cain calls the 'extrovert ideal' that it is missing out on the talents of half its population. If you can't speak in public, wilt in meetings and hate networking, then you are an introvert and you are destined to be ignored by an attention-deficit world. Cain argues – correctly, I think – that this is mad. It is a strong point and she brings in serious data to back it up. In the end, though, her insistence that one of two sizes fits all means that this book becomes little more than another Men Are From Mars, Women Are From Venus tick-box work. People are more complicated, subtle and surprising than these either-or classifications. And not every introvert is an unrecognised genius, nor every extrovert an idiot thug.

D Recognising the complexity of human nature, the author of *Quiet* avoids falling into the trap of labelling introversion and extroversion as a clearly-defined distinction. Instead, Susan Cain's approach is to treat them as two extremes on a scale that covers a whole range of personality types, each with its own particular characteristics. Unlike others who have published works on this topic, she makes no judgment on the relative merits of tending towards one of these extremes or the other, and in fact calls for greater objectivity when assessing the weaker and stronger points of extroverts and introverts. That in itself is one reason why this perceptive and consistently readable book is particularly likely to appeal to those who regard themselves as belonging to the latter group.

7 Use the context to work out the meanings of these phrasal verbs.

1 set up (A)
2 play out (B)
3 play down (B)
4 miss out on (B & C)
5 back up (C)
6 call for (D)

8 Complete the sentences with the correct forms of the phrasal verbs in Exercise 7.

1 The firm tried to .... the harmful effects of very loud noise on factory workers.
2 The story of good triumphing over evil has been .... in so many films.
3 Advice about the need to get enough sleep is .... by recent research.
4 The government has .... an enquiry into the serious problem of online bullying.
5 The victims of the accident have .... an enquiry into its causes.
6 People who don't take part in social activities .... a lot of fun.

10 GRAMMAR

Wishes and regrets   Ⓖ *Page 97*

1 👁 Correct the mistakes in these sentences written by exam candidates. In each case explain why it is wrong.

1 Instead of looking for solutions to life's problems, we just wish they disappear.
2 I think it is time that we consider changing the time of our meetings.
3 If only did tourists show more respect when they visit our country.
4 I'd rather my father was with me when I was a child, but he often had to work abroad.
5 I wish I could spend longer in that village, but I didn't have time for everything.
6 Our office uses very old software and I think it's time we should change it.
7 Kate wished she wouldn't have looked at those photos because what she saw shocked her.
8 It's high time you to come to visit me here because I know you need to relax.

2 Underline the correct option in each sentence.

1 It's high time you and I *will have / had / are having* a serious talk about our relationship.
2 If only I *didn't have / hadn't / wouldn't have* to take the bus every morning.
3 I wish that firm *stopped / would stop / will stop* phoning me all the time.
4 It's time Kyle *sought / seeks / had sought* specialist advice for his condition.
5 We'd rather *you'd / you would've / you've* asked permission before you took the day off.
6 I wish I *would / could / might* remember people's names better.
7 Amelia wishes she *didn't spend / hadn't spent / wouldn't have spent* so much yesterday.
8 Don't you wish you *were / could be / was* able to read people's minds?

3 Complete the second sentence so that it has a similar meaning to the first sentence.

1 Jake knows that he shouldn't have lied to them.
Jake wishes that .... a lie.
2 It's a pity you didn't contact me about this sooner.
I'd rather .... touch with me about this sooner.
3 I would so much like to be able to speak Spanish fluently.
If only .... Spanish.
4 Zoe should have realised before now that she needs to work harder if she wants to pass.
It's high time Zoe .... a greater effort if she wants to pass.
5 The Minister regretted causing such controversy by his speech.
The Minister wished that .... controversial speech.
6 Joe keeps asking me for loans, which is really annoying.
I really wish Joe .... him money.

4 What would you say in these situations? Write two sentences for each, using the prompt.

1 You spent all night revising, but now you can't stay awake in the exam. (wish)
2 Whenever you go out in your friend's car, it breaks down. (it's time)
3 You see a fantastic but ridiculously expensive holiday advertised. (if only)
4 A company keeps sending you junk email. (wish)
5 You don't want your friends to call round at your house too early. (would rather)
6 You said something unkind to a friend and now they won't speak to you. (if only)
7 There was a great concert last weekend but you couldn't go. (wish)
8 By the end of the week, you haven't got enough money to go out with your friends. (it's time)

10 READING AND USE OF ENGLISH

Three-part phrasal verbs

1 Replace the underlined words with the correct form of these C1-level phrasal verbs. Add pronouns where necessary.

> brush up on   check up on   come up against
> do away with   get back to   get through to
> read up on   stand up to

1 When I have time, I want to <u>study some books about</u> child psychology.
2 Some people <u>find they have to deal with</u> discrimination when they apply for jobs.
3 I'll <u>be in touch with</u> you later with more information.
4 The boss is always <u>trying to discover what I'm doing</u> while I'm working.
5 I need to <u>improve the level of</u> my Spanish.
6 You should <u>defend yourself against</u> bullies.
7 When Luke is in this kind of mood, it's difficult to <u>make him understand</u>.
8 It's high time they <u>abolished</u> the minimum age limit to become President.

2 Complete the phrasal verbs by adding one word from A and B. The words can be used more than once.

> A: away   down   out   round   up
> B: from   of   on   to   with

1 Young people often look .... successful adults as role models.
2 Sadly, Alice seems to have fallen .... Maria.
3 The doctor advised me to cut .... sugar.
4 Parents often tell their children to stay .... kids who misbehave.
5 My brother made an excuse to get .... helping with the housework.
6 I keep meaning to visit my aunt, but I never actually get .... it.
7 I'm not surprised Anna's so stressed. She has a lot to put .... at home.
8 Safety officials are investigating the events that led .... the accident.

> **Exam tip**
>
> If you can't think of the whole answer, write what you can – you might get one mark.

Part 4

> **Quick steps to Reading and Use of English Part 4**
> • Decide if the sentence is positive or negative.
> • Write only the missing words and the key word.
> • Check your spelling. You lose marks for mistakes.

3 Look at the exam task and answer these questions. Then do the exam task.

1 Which words in the example (**0**) do you think get marks?
2 What does each question mainly test?

Exam task

For questions **1–6**, complete the second sentence so that it has a similar meaning to the first sentence, using the word given. **Do not change the word given.** You must use between **three** and **six** words, including the word given. Here is an example (**0**).

Example:

0 I advise you not to get involved in that argument.
STAY
If I were you, I WOULD STAY OUT OF that argument.

1 We really should get someone to repair the printer.
HIGH
It's .... repaired.

2 In this town, very few drivers escape punishment for illegal parking.
AWAY
In this town, hardly .... parking illegally.

3 I think it would be better if Mr Jay could make an immediate decision.
MIND
I would rather .... immediately.

4 I succeeded in persuading Jo not to quit her job.
TALK
I managed .... her job.

5 The manager now regrets not picking Lionel for the team.
LEFT
The manager now wishes that he .... the team.

6 The Government's policy has been strongly criticised recently.
COME
The Government's policy has .... recently.

Personality adjectives

1 In small groups, discuss these questions.

    1 Read the C1-level adjectives that describe personality in the box below. Which usually have positive meanings, and which negative? Which can be either?

    2 What is the opposite of each adjective?

> anti-social conscientious cool courageous
> extrovert idealistic imaginative insecure
> insensitive modest naïve natural
> narrow-minded outgoing self-centred
> self-conscious talkative trustworthy
> unconventional well-balanced

2 Think of celebrities, or characters from films or TV shows, that six of these adjectives could describe. Ask your partner if they agree.

Part 4

Quick steps to Listening Part 4
- Remember that speakers may say things that distract you from the right answer.
- If you have to correct one of your answers, make sure it hasn't led to other mistakes.
- Never leave a blank. Always make an intelligent guess.

3 Look at the exam task. What does Task One focus on? What is the focus of Task Two?

4 Note down words and phrases associated with the reasons for choosing each job in Task 1 and each kind of personality in Task 2.

5 🔘 **2.14** Do the exam task. Listen for words and meanings from Exercise 4.

Exam task

You will hear five short extracts in which five people are talking about their jobs and personalities.

While you listen you must complete both tasks.

TASK ONE

For questions **1–5**, choose from the list (**A–H**) the reason each speaker gives for choosing their current occupation.

A to work regular hours	
B to go into the family business	
C to make use of their qualifications	Speaker 1 [1]
D to help people experiencing difficulties	Speaker 2 [2]
E to take on a challenge	Speaker 3 [3]
F to gain experience in a particular field	Speaker 4 [4]
G to use their creative abilities	Speaker 5 [5]
H to obtain financial rewards	

TASK TWO

For questions **6–10**, choose from the list (**A–H**) the way each speaker describes their own personality.

A ambitious	
B extrovert	Speaker 1 [6]
C idealistic	Speaker 2 [7]
D conscientious	
E pessimistic	Speaker 3 [8]
F emotional	Speaker 4 [9]
G sociable	
H open-minded	Speaker 5 [10]

Exam tip ›

Don't worry if a speaker uses a word you don't know. You may not need to understand it to do the task.

10 SPEAKING

Reaching a decision

1 In Speaking Part 3, which expressions would you use for each of 1–5 below?

a Another way of looking at it would be …
b So we're agreed, then.
c I think I'd go for …
d Yes, but don't you think …
e Let's leave it at that, shall we?
f OK, which shall we have?
g I'd be in favour of …
h That's the one we'll choose, then.
i Which do you think would be best?
j Let's just agree to disagree.

1 suggesting which to choose
2 asking your partner to choose
3 trying to change your partner's opinion
4 saying you both agree
5 saying you can't agree

Parts 3 & 4   *Page 109-111*

Quick steps to Speaking Part 3
- During the last minute, try to reach a decision with your partner through negotiation.
- If you can't agree, say so, e.g. *OK, I don't think we'll reach agreement on that point.*

2 Read the exam task instructions. What do you have to talk about first? What do you then have to decide?

Exam task

Here are some ways people can reduce the amount of stress in their daily lives and a question for you to discuss. First you have some time to look at the task. Now, talk to each other about how useful these methods might be in helping people reduce stress in their daily lives.

How useful might these methods be in helping people reduce stress in their daily lives?

- taking up a hobby
- doing regular exercise
- listening to relaxing music
- taking regular breaks from work or study
- turning off the mobile phone and computer

Now you have about a minute to decide which method would be the most effective in helping people reduce everyday stress.

Exam tip

When the test is over, say goodbye but don't ask the examiners to comment on your speaking. They're not allowed to.

3 ◉ **2.15** Listen to Alina and Ivan practising the second section of Part 3. Answer these questions.
1 Which method are they discussing?
2 Do they agree in the end?

4 ◉ **2.15** Listen to Alina and Ivan again. Which expressions from Exercise 1 do they use?

5 Work in groups of three. Look at the Quick steps to Speaking Part 3, then do both parts of the exam task twice. Take turns as 'examiner'. Try to reach a decision each time.

Quick steps to Speaking Part 4
- If your partner is talking a lot and you feel it is your turn, interrupt very politely.
- Add more points and keep talking until the examiner says 'thank you'.

6 Stay in your groups. Look at the Quick steps to Speaking Part 4 and do Part 4 three times.

- Ask the 'candidates' three questions, if necessary prompting with follow-up questions such as *Why?* or *Do you agree?*
- Stop them after five minutes and comment on how well they did the task.

List of questions for Speaking Part 4

1 Do you think life is more stressful today than it was 50 years ago?
2 What are some of the consequences of stress in people's lives?
3 Do you think the amount of noise in present-day urban living is a cause of stress?
4 How important is it for people to achieve a balance between work and leisure in their lives?
5 Some people say our concern with success in life leads to stress. What is your opinion?
6 Do you think people sleep too little or too much these days?
7 Can anxiety sometimes be a good thing, for instance before an exam or doing sports?
8 How important is it for people to have a long holiday every year?
9 Nowadays, money is the greatest cause of anxiety. To what extent do you agree?

Concession

1 Complete each sentence with one of the words in the box. Underline any fixed phrases they form.

> how may same so wherever
> whichever who yet

1 You can call me in the evening, no matter .... late it is.
2 Leah is quite a calm person. Even .... , she occasionally becomes impatient.
3 It .... be the most expensive perfume on the market, but it certainly isn't the best.
4 He can wait in the queue like everyone else, no matter .... he is.
5 The sound quality wasn't perfect, but we enjoyed the concert all the ....
6 You can choose a red, green or blue card, ... you prefer.
7 Jordan rarely smiles, and .... I think he's quite happy with life.
8 Lucy's dog Vanilla always travelled with her, ... she went.

2 Rewrite the sentences using the expression in brackets.

1 You can say anything you like but I won't change my mind. (whatever)
2 Jessica carried on working, but she was obviously exhausted by then. (even so)
3 It makes no difference where you go, this phone lets you stay in touch. (no matter)
4 The TV critics say it's a wonderful series, but I still think it's boring. (however)
5 Nobody's heard of Ethan James, even though he's a brilliant artist. (and yet)
6 Although the talk was rather long, the speaker made some good points. (all the same)
7 Despite being unable to recall names, Max has an excellent memory for numbers. (may)
8 Amy doesn't care what people say, she'll keep on doing what she feels is right. (no matter)

3 Complete the sentences with your own ideas.

1 Young people nowadays are influenced by the media, wherever ....
2 Everyone should receive a good education, no matter ....
3 Someone may seem very intelligent, but ....
4 Two children in a family can have exactly the same upbringing. Even so, ...
5 Some adults didn't do well at school, and yet ....
6 Throughout life people continue learning, however ....

Part 1: essay   Page 99

> **Quick steps to writing a Part 1 essay**
> • In your introduction, comment generally on the topic and indicate the content of your essay.
> • In your closing paragraph, try to leave the reader with something to think about.
> • Make sure any corrections you make are clear.

4 Look at the exam task instructions and the first three notes. Answer these questions.

1 What do you have to write about, and for whom?
2 Which points must you choose from?
3 What must you also write about two of those points?

5 Look at the first Quick step, then read these three possible opening paragraphs for this essay. Which is best? Why?

A   There are clearly a number of factors, or influences, that can help determine an individual's personality. In this essay I shall deal with two of the most important: genetics and society in general.

B   The issue of how a person's character is formed has long been controversial. The main division is between those who claim personality traits are inherited, and those who believe they are shaped by the social environment in which they live.

C   Personality can be defined as all the attitudes, beliefs, emotions, thoughts and qualities that distinguish one person from another. Clearly the differences between individuals can be enormous, but what are the forces that shape their character?

Write your answer in **220–260** words in an appropriate style.
You have watched a discussion on factors that help determine an individual's personality. You have made the notes below:

Influences that determine personality:
- genetics
- family life
- society in general

Some opinions expressed in the discussion:

"Just as physical characteristics come from our genes, so do psychological ones."

"Children imitate their parents' behaviour and eventually become similar people."

"School life has an enormous role in forming a child's character."

Write an essay for your tutor discussing **two** of the factors in your notes. You should **explain which factor you think is more important in determining personality, giving reasons** to support your opinion. You may, if you wish, make use of the opinions expressed in the discussion, but you should use your own words as far as possible.

The so-called nature versus nurture debate is one of the most divisive in Psychology. On the one hand, some maintain that our personality and consequently our behaviour are the result of inherited characteristics, while others believe we are entirely the product of society.

According to the latter, the human mind at birth is a complete blank which later develops certain traits as a result of life's experiences. Of particular importance is the school environment, where the child's way of interacting, their response to rules and how they are treated by others all help shape their character. Society's values also play a significant part. For instance, certain cultures encourage individuals to cooperate, whereas in others the emphasis is on competition.

In contrast, some scientists claim that our DNA not only determines attributes like our height or life expectancy, it also affects traits such as how open, extrovert or conscientious we are. They believe we are born destined to grow into a certain kind of person with certain abilities, no matter what our environment. Others on the 'nature' side of the argument include Freud, who believed humans to be innately aggressive, and Chomsky, who stated we are born with a set of innate rules for learning language.

My own view is that we may have inborn characteristics and abilities, but their modification by our environment is an even more powerful force. Siblings, however similar their DNA, often have completely different personalities. And recent research indicates that having a good sense of humour is learned from those around us, not determined genetically.

6 Read the model essay opposite and answer these questions.

1 Which two of the notes does the writer use, and in which paragraphs?
2 Which two handwritten opinions does he use, and how does he paraphrase them?
3 Which factor does he think is more important and what reasons does he give?
4 Which concession links does he use?

7 You are going to do the exam task. If you intend to write about family life, get ideas by thinking about these points and making notes.

- A child's emotions, both positive and negative, develop as a result of interacting with parents, and with siblings if they have them.
- Qualities such as intellectual curiosity, sociability and self-confidence can be encouraged or discouraged by parents.
- Family structures can vary widely between and within cultures.
- Studies of twins seem to show that their personalities remain very similar wherever they live and whoever they live with.

8 Look at all the Quick steps, then plan and write your essay. When you have finished, check your work as in Unit 1, Writing Exercise 8 on page 15.

Exam tip

Show where one paragraph ends and another begins, either by leaving a line between them or indenting.

GRAMMAR REFERENCE

Unit 1 Review of verb tenses

Referring to the present

The **present simple** is used

1 to refer to routine actions or habits:
*Stefan **goes** to the cinema most weekends.*

2 to refer to repeated events:
*Tropical storms often **occur** in the Caribbean.*

3 to show that a situation is regarded as permanent:
*Sarah **works** for a small TV production company. (It's a permanent job.)*

4 to show that something is always true, or a definite fact:
*Two and two **make** four.*

The **present continuous** is used

1 to describe an action which is happening now:
*This storm **is causing** damage all over the country.*

2 for a temporary situation:
*I'm **using** Jack's car while he's on holiday.*

3 for changes or developing situations:
*The number of hurricanes **is increasing** year on year.*

4 with *always* or *forever* to express irritation:
*The editor **is** always/forever **making** me rewrite the articles I submit.*

! The present continuous is normally used with active verbs:
*The editor **is talking** to the sports journalists at the moment.*

It is not normally used with **stative verbs** (which describe a state, such as existing or feeling):
~~*The head of the TV channel isn't believing this programme is too controversial to be broadcast.*~~
*The head of the TV channel **believes** this programme is too controversial to be broadcast.* √

However, some stative verbs can be used in the present continuous when they describe actions:
*What **are** you **having** for lunch?*
Here, *have* is used as an active verb, meaning to eat.

The **present perfect** is used

1 to refer to the present result of a past action or event:
*I can't phone for an ambulance – **I've lost** my mobile.*

2 to show that an event or action that started in the past has continued until the present:
*Thousands of homes **have been built** in this town in the last few years, and many more are planned.*

3 to refer to an event or action that happened at an unspecified time in a period up to now:
*I've **seen** that film already. (the period is my life up to the present)*

4 to focus on the number of times an action has been repeated:
*I've **read** this article ten times and I still don't understand it.*

The **present perfect continuous** is used to refer to an event or action that started in the past and has continued until the present. While the present perfect focuses on a completed action, the present perfect continuous usually focuses on one that is ongoing:
*I've **written** the article. **(It's finished.)***
*I've **been writing** the article all morning. **(It probably isn't finished.)***

Referring to the past

The **past simple** is used for past events, actions or habits:
*We last **experienced** a tropical storm only a week ago.*
*I always **watched** the TV news when I lived abroad.*

It is normally used with a specific time reference (*a week ago, in 2010, when I lived abroad*).

The **past continuous** is used

1 to show a continued action which was happening when another action took place:
*The magazine was launched just when the sales of news magazines **were falling**.*
*The phone rang when I **was watching** an interesting documentary on TV. (I may or may not have stopped watching to answer the phone.)*

2 to refer to two actions happening at the same time in the past:
*While some journalists **were discussing** the latest developments, others **were watching** the breaking news online.*

The **past perfect** is used to show that an action happened earlier than another past action; it makes the sequence of events clear:
*I didn't watch the programme about hurricanes on TV last night, because I'd already **seen** a similar programme. (I saw the similar programme before last night's programme was shown.)*

The **past perfect continuous** is used

1 to refer to an action that happened during a period leading up to another past action:
*The newspaper **had been losing** so much money that the owner decided to close it down.*

2 to show how long an action continued until a certain point in the past:
*The reporters **had been following** the film star for days before they were able to interview her.*

Used to / didn't use to + **infinitive** and *would* + **infinitive** are used

1   to refer to repeated actions or habits in the past that are no longer the case:
    *Before digital cameras were invented, people **used to take** / **would take** photos on film.*
    *When I was a teenager, I **didn't use to take** many photos, but now I do.*

2   to refer to a past state. *Would* cannot be used here:
    *This **used to be** a very quiet neighbourhood.*
    ~~*This **would be** a very quiet neighbourhood.*~~

Used to is not normally used with time expressions specifying the duration of the action:
    *I **used to live** in Edinburgh before I moved to London.*
    *I **lived** in Edinburgh for five years before I moved to London.*
    ~~*I used to live in Edinburgh for five years before I moved to London.*~~

Referring to the future

will + **infinitive** (the future simple) is used

1   to predict the future:
    *Aftershocks from yesterday's earthquake **will** probably **continue** for several days.*

2   to express a decision that has just been made, usually by the speaker:
    *I know! We'**ll go** to the Science Museum.*

3   to express the speaker's insistence on doing something:
    *We **will find** somewhere better to live – I promise you.*

going to + **infinitive** is used

1   for decisions or intentions about the future:
    *The owner of the local bookshop **is going to invite** a well-known author to give a talk.* (The speaker is reporting what the owner has decided to do.)

2   for predictions about the future based on evidence, or to refer to the outcome of a process that has already started:
    *You drive much too fast. You'**re going to have** an accident one of these days.*
    *My sister'**s going to have** a baby at the end of March.*

The **present continuous** is used to refer to something already arranged:
*We'**re meeting** the journalist tomorrow morning.*

The **present simple** is used for future events fixed by a timetable or schedule:
    *The sun **rises** at 5.30 tomorrow.*
    *The next train **is** at 11 o'clock.*

The **future continuous** is used

1   for temporary actions in progress at a particular time in the future:
    *This time next week, we'**ll be flying** to Brazil.*

2   to ask about the listener's plans, often to lead on to a request:
    *Will you **be going** out this evening? If not, can I come round and see you?*

The **future perfect** is used

1   for actions in a period up to a particular time in the future:
    *The oil spill **will have caused** a lot of damage by the time the flow from the ship can be stopped.*

2   for actions which will be completed before a particular time in the future:
    *I'**ll have finished lunch** long before you arrive.*

The **future perfect continuous** is used for actions in a period up to a particular time in the future, emphasising the length of time:
    *At the beginning of next March, I'**ll have been working** in the same job for 17 years.*

In **time and conditional clauses referring to the future** *will* is not normally used to refer to the future. Instead, present tenses (simple, continuous and perfect) are used:
    *If the volcano **erupts**, the surrounding area will be badly affected.* (not ~~will erupt~~)
    I'll ring you at 7p.m. unless you're having dinner then. (not ~~will be having~~)
    *As soon as the flood water **has receded**, the residents will start clearing up their homes.* (not ~~will have receded~~)

Unit 2 Participle clauses

The **present participle active (*-ing*)** is used to make a statement where the subject is omitted because it is the same as the subject of the main clause. The events of the two clauses can relate to each other in various ways:

1   cause and effect; the participle clause, which states the cause, normally comes first:
    ***Realising** the mountain top was covered in mist, we decided to turn back.* (= Because we realised …)

2   description of the subject of the main clause; the participle clause normally comes second:
    *The volunteers arrived at the clinic **feeling** a little nervous.*

3   two simultaneous events with the same subject; the participle clause normally comes second:
    *The woman hurried after her dog, **calling** to him to come back.*

4 one event happening during another; the longer event is in the participle clause, which normally comes second:
*The new volunteer hurt himself (while) **playing** football.*

The **perfect participle, active (having -ed)** is used to show that the event of the participle clause happened first. The clauses can be in either order:
***Having eaten** all the food it could find in the camp, the bear wandered away.*

The **perfect participle, passive (having been -ed)** is used when the action of the participle clause happens before the action of the main clause. The participle clause usually comes first:
***Having been attacked** during his previous visit, he was very careful about where he went.*

The **past participle (-ed)** has a passive meaning. The participle clause usually comes first. It can express

1 cause:
***Ignored** by the other children, the boy played by himself.*
(= Because he was ignored …)

2 description:
***Surrounded** on three sides by mountains, the village rarely enjoys much sunshine.*

3 condition:
***Kept** in a cool place, yoghurt will remain fresh for a long time.* (= If yoghurt is kept in a cool place …)

Unit 3 Reported speech

In **reported speech** the full meaning needs to be understood and conveyed in the report, including references to time and place. In these, *say* is used, however, many other verbs are available, such as *suggest, whisper, protest, claim*, etc.

Tense changes ('backshifting')

When direct speech is reported using a past tense (e.g., *She said …*), other verbs often change, e.g. present tenses are replaced by the corresponding tense in the past.

1 Present simple to past simple:
*'My flatmate **is** very untidy.'*
*He said his flatmate **was** very untidy.*

2 Present continuous to past continuous:
*'Amelia **is making** some hot chocolate.'*
*He said Amelia **was making** some hot chocolate.*

3 Present perfect to past perfect:
*'My flatmate **has become** my best friend.'*
*She said that her flatmate **had become** her best friend.*

4 Present perfect continuous to past perfect continuous:
*'I've **been looking** for an affordable flat for six months.'*
*She said she'**d been looking** for an affordable flat for six months.*

5 Past simple to past perfect:
*'I **went** to Peru for a year before going to university.'*
*She said she **had been** to Peru for a year before going to university.*
Backshifting is not essential here:
*She said she **went** to Peru for a year before going to university.*

6 *Can* to *could, will* to *would, must* to *had to*
'Jack can speak three languages fluently.'
*She said Jack **could** speak three languages fluently.*

'I'll be in touch within a week.'
*He said he **would** be in touch within a week.*

*'You **must** apply for a visa before your trip.'*
*He said I **had to** apply for a visa before my trip.*

Backshifting is usually avoided
1 if the reporting verb is in the present tense:
*'I **hope** to visit my parents.'*
*She says she **hopes** to visit her parents.*

2 if what is reported is still true:
*'I'm **going** to have a baby next month.'*
*She said she'**s going** to have a baby next month.*

3 when the modal verbs *would, should, might, could* and *ought to* are reported:
*'John **could** already have arrived.'*
*He said that John **could** already have arrived.*

Reported questions

These use the word order subject-verb, just as in statements, and there is no question mark:
*'**Is** this your usual way of spending the evening?'*
*He asked me if **this was** my usual way of spending the evening.*

*'Where'**s** your car?'*
*He asked me where **my car was**.*

Reported requests

Requests that use *will, can* or *may* are reported using *would, could* or (rarely) *might*. The word order is subject-verb, just as in statements, and there is no question mark.
*'**Will** you lend me your book?'*
*She asked me if I **would lend** her my book.*

Reported commands

Commands are usually reported using *tell, order* or *command* and the infinitive of the main verb:

'**Call** for an ambulance at once.'
He **told me to call** for an ambulance at once.
'**Don't give** the children any sweets.'
She **told me not to give** the children any sweets.'

Time references

If *today, this evening, tonight,* etc. in direct speech are reported when the day is in the past, *that day/evening/night* is used:

'I'm going to the cinema **this evening**.'
She said she was going to the cinema **that evening**.

If *tomorrow* in direct speech is reported when that day is in the past, *the next/following day* is used instead:

'I'm going to Vietnam **tomorrow**.'
She said she was going to Vietnam **the next/following day**.

Similarly, *next week* is replaced by the *next/following week*.

Yesterday and *last week* are reported as *the previous day/week* or *the day/week before*:

'I started a new job last week.'
She said she had started a new job **the previous week/the week before**.

Place references

References to places depend on the precise meaning of what is reported:

'I'm very happy **here**.'
can be reported as
Sally said she was very happy **there**. (the speaker is in a different place from Sally) OR
Sally said she was very happy **here**. (the speaker is in the same place)
Note that if Sally is *still* happy, the reported verb will be *is*:
Sally said she's very happy **here/there**.

Unit 4 Passive

The passive is used only with transitive verbs, that is, verbs that take an object:

Phil and I **asked focus groups** to try out early prototypes.
In the passive this becomes:
Focus groups **were asked** to try out early prototypes.

Intransitive verbs, such as *appear, happen* cannot be used in the passive.

The passive is often used in fairly formal writing, such as news reports, and academic, scientific and technical writing:

1 to describe part of a process:
   Orders **are delivered** within 48 hours.
2 to emphasise the object rather than the subject:
   The book **was completed** when the novelist was in her 80s.
3 to state a rule or make a polite request:
   Identity badges **must be worn** at all times.
4 to say what people tend to expect, believe, etc.:
   It **is thought** that the invention will be very successful.
5 to indicate that we don't know who did something:
   These houses **were built** in the 1960s.
6 to indicate that we don't know who said something:
   The company **is said** to have made a loss of nearly $1 million.

If a passive includes the agent of the action, this normally comes at the end of the sentence, and follows *by*:

That was invented **by** my tutor!

Phrasal verbs are not split in the passive:

Every tenth vehicle **was pulled over** by the police so they could check its tyres.

Forming the passive with *be*

The passive is normally formed using the verb *be* in an appropriate tense, plus the past participle of the main verb. In passive sentences, the tense of *be* is the same as the tense in the corresponding active sentence:

Tense	Active	Passive
Present simple	We sell ready-to-cook meals.	Ready-to-cook meals are sold.
Present continuous	We are selling ready-to-cook meals.	Ready-to-cook meals are being sold.
Present perfect	We have sold ready-to-cook meals.	Ready-to-cook meals have been sold.
Past simple	We sold ready-to-cook meals.	Ready-to-cook meals were sold.
Past continuous	We were selling ready-to-cook meals.	Ready-to-cook meals were being sold.
Past perfect	We had sold ready-to-cook meals.	Ready-to-cook meals had been sold.
Future simple	We will sell ready-to-cook meals.	Ready-to-cook meals will be sold.

Future continuous (the passive is rarely used)	We will be selling ready-to-cook meals.	Ready-to-cook meals will be being sold.
Future perfect	We will have sold ready-to-cook meals.	Ready-to-cook meals will have been sold.
Going to future	We are going to sell ready-to-cook meals.	Ready-to-cook meals are going to be sold.
Modal verbs	We can/could/ would/should/ may/might/must sell ready-to-cook meals.	Ready-to-cook meals can/could/ would/should/ may/might/must be sold.
Need	We need to sell ready-to-cook meals.	Ready-to-cook meals need to be sold/need selling.
Modal perfect	We could/would/ should/may/ might/must have sold ready-to-cook meals.	Ready-to-cook meals could/ would/should/ may/might/must have been sold.

Forming the passive with *get*

The passive is sometimes formed with *get*, most often in informal, spoken English:

> There wasn't room on the stall for all the meals, so a few **got left** in the van.

If an adverb is used as part of the verb phrase, it follows *be* but precedes *get*:

> The retailer's loyalty card **was finally launched** in 2002.
> The retailer's loyalty card **finally got launched** in 2002.

The causative *have* and *get*

To have something done (or more informally, *to get something done*) can mean that the subject of the sentence causes the action to be done:

> Alex and Phil **had / got** their business plan **checked** before they showed it to the bank.

With *get*, this structure is also used when the subject of the sentence carries out the action:

> They needed to **get** the stall **set** up before the market opened.

Get is used to give a sense of urgency:

> Stephanie needs to **get** her car **repaired**.

Have, but not *get*, can also be used to refer to an experience (usually bad) that happened to the subject of the sentence:

> Alex and Phil **had** the day's takings **stolen**.

Impersonal passives with verbs like *think, claim, say, believe, consider, expect, know, report,* etc.

These allow us to give an opinion as if it was a general feeling, rather than a personal one.

1 *It* + *be* is an impersonal way of introducing our attitudes and feelings without mentioning ourselves:
   They think that the public is losing confidence in cheques. (active)
   It is thought that the public is losing confidence in cheques. (passive)

2 The subject of the finite clause can become the subject of the passive sentence, using an infinitive:
   People believe that money is a source of happiness. (active)
   It is believed that money is a source of happiness. (passive with it)
   *Money is believed **to be** a source of happiness.* (passive with the subject of the clause – *money* – as subject of the sentence followed by infinitive)

   People know that the company is losing money.
   It is known that the company is losing money. (passive with *it*)
   *The company is known **to be losing** money.* (passive with the subject of the clause – *the company* – as subject of the sentence)

Make and *let*

Make + object + infinitive without *to* requires *to* in the passive:

> The thieves **made the shopkeeper open** the safe. (active)
> The shopkeeper **was made to open** the safe. (passive)

Let + object + infinitive has no passive form. Instead *be allowed to* is used:

> The tutor **let me leave** when I had finished my essay. (active)
> I **was allowed to leave** when I had finished my essay. (passive)

Unit 5 Conditional forms

Conditional clauses are used to show that one circumstance or set of circumstances depends on another:

> If you **look after** your health, you**'ll reduce** the risk of developing certain diseases.
> It will be easy to get to the conference on time if you go by train.

Note a comma is used after the conditional clause. *Unless* (i.e 'if ... not') or *Providing / Provided (that)* (i.e 'if and only if') can also be used to start a conditional clause.

1. **Zero conditional** is used for something that is timeless or generally true:
   *If water **is boiled**, it **turns** into steam.*
   *Water **doesn't turn** into steam unless it's **boiled**.*

2. **First conditional** is used for a possibility in the present or future:
   If that's Kevin on the phone, I'll talk to him. (The conditional clause refers to the present.)
   *If you **take** a painkiller before you go to bed, you **may feel** better in the morning.* (The conditional clause refers to the future.)
   Would like is sometimes used in the conditional clause of a polite request:
   If you'd like to follow me, I'll take you to the doctor's office.

3. **Second conditional** is used for something hypothetical, unlikely, impossible or not true in the present or future; the condition is not expected to be fulfilled:
   *If you **took** this medicine, it **would cure** you.* (I don't expect that you'll take the medicine.)
   *If I **were/was** you, I wouldn't wait much longer.* (I'm not you.)
   The **second conditional** is used in tentative, polite requests:
   *I **would be** grateful if you **gave** me further details of what gym membership involves.*

4. **Third conditional** is used for something in the past that is hypothetical, not true:
   *If Carl **hadn't been** so fit, he **would have taken** much longer to recover.* (He was very fit, so he recovered quickly.)

5. **Mixed conditionals** most commonly use parts of the second and third conditionals:
   *If **you'd seen** the doctor sooner, **you'd be** much healthier now.* (Something in the present that results from something in the past – mixed third and second conditionals.)
   *If she **was/were** a doctor, she **would have been** able to help you.* (She isn't a doctor so couldn't help you in the past – mixed second and third conditionals.)

6. In fairly formal language, *the conditional clause* can begin with inversion of the subject and auxiliary verb *was / were / had / should*, instead of using *if*:
   If you were to train regularly, your running speed would improve.
   ***Were you** to train regularly, your running speed would improve.* (more formal)
   If it rains heavily, the race will be cancelled.
   ***Should it rain** heavily, the race will be cancelled.* (more formal)

Unit 6 Verbs followed by the infinitive and/or -ing

Sometimes the object of a verb is another verb, rather than a noun phrase.

1. Verbs followed by *to* + infinitive include: *afford, agree, appear, arrange, ask, attempt, choose, dare, decide, expect, fail, hope, learn, manage, need, offer, pretend, promise, refuse, seem, struggle, tend, threaten, want, would like*:
   *Filmed concerts **struggle to convey** the tension of live performance.*
   *Many people **want to see** a band but are put off by high ticket prices.*

2. Verbs followed by object + *to* + infinitive include: *advise, allow, ask, enable, encourage, **expect**, force, invite, **need**, persuade, remind, teach, tell, **want**, **would like**.* Those in bold can also be used intransitively (see 1 above):
   *Art collections on the Internet **enable everyone to study** them from home.*
   *My father **taught me to ride** a bike.*
   *Jackie **wanted me to see** his favourite band.* (note *want*, along with other verbs, can be used in more than one group – see 1 above)

3. Verbs followed by object + infinitive without *to* include: *make, let.*
   *The actors **let me take** some photos of them.*
   *When I was a child, my parents **made me do** my homework as soon as I got home from school.*

4. Verbs followed by *-ing* include: *admit, avoid, bother, can't bear, can't stand, deny, dislike, enjoy, finish, hate, imagine, involve, keep, miss, mind, suggest.*
   *I **enjoy seeing** sculptures and paintings online.*

5. Verbs ending with a preposition are always followed by an *-ing* form, e.g. *break off, carry on, get round to, give up, insist on, look forward to, take on, think about.*
   *After seeing the museum's collection online, I **looked forward to visiting** the museum in person.*

6. Verbs followed by object + *-ing* include verbs relating to the senses, e.g. *feel, hear, see, smell, watch*:
   *I **watched the band giving** a stunning performance.*
   *If I **hear people talking** on their mobile phones at a gig, I just want to leave.*

7. Verbs followed by either *to* + infinitive or the *-ing* form, with the same meaning include: *begin, bother, can't bear, continue, hate, intend, like, love, prefer, start.*
   *Many people **like to join** in the singing.*
   *Many people **like joining** in the singing.*

Sometimes there is a slight difference in meaning:
*I **like going** to the dentist.* (I enjoy it.)
*I **like to go** to the dentist on my way to work.* (This is my preference, but it doesn't necessarily mean that I enjoy my visits to the dentist.)

8   Verbs followed by either *to* + infinitive or the *-ing* form, with different meanings include: *forget, go on, mean, regret, remember, stop, try*:
*I'll never **forget seeing** Botticelli's painting The Birth of Venus for the first time.* (I actually saw the painting, and I'll never forget that experience.)
*I **forgot to see** The Birth of Venus when I went to Florence.* (I intended to see it, but I forgot to.)
*Fiona **went on visiting** the Museo Reina Sofia website until she had seen everything.* (She didn't stop until she'd seen everything.)
*Fiona **went on to visit** the Museo Reina Sofia website.* (She finished what she was doing, then visited the Museo website.)
*Going to the Uffizi **meant queuing** outside for a couple of hours.* (Going to the Uffizi involved queuing.)
*We **meant to see** the new museum, but there wasn't enough time.* (We intended to see it, but didn't.)
*We **regret informing** you about the error, as it has obviously caused you considerable anxiety.* (We informed you, but now we are sorry we did so.)
*We **regret to inform** you that the concert has been cancelled.* (We are sorry for what we are about to do.)
*I can **remember going** to the theatre for the first time.* (I went to the theatre and now I clearly remember it.)
*I **remembered to go** to the bank.* (I remembered that I had to go to the bank, and then I went there.)
*Tom **stopped drinking** coffee when he realised it kept him awake.* (He used to drink coffee, but now he doesn't.)
*Sheila **stopped to make** some coffee.* (Sheila stopped whatever she was doing in order to make some coffee.)
*I **tried looking** in the garden, but I still couldn't find my keys.* (I looked in the garden hoping to find my keys.)
*I **tried to look** for my glasses, but I felt too ill to move.* (I wanted to look for my glasses, but couldn't.)

Unit 7 Inversion of subject and verb

Inversion means having a verb, usually an auxiliary, before the subject of a sentence as in questions:
***Have** the nature reserve guards caught the illegal hunters?*

Inversion is also used

1   to emphasise an adverbial phrase, normally one that is negative in meaning, e.g. *only, no sooner, not once, never, rarely, seldom, scarcely, hardly, little, few, under no circumstances*:

The tourists had no sooner arrived than they noticed some giraffes in the distance. (Without inversion.)
*No sooner **had the tourists** arrived than they noticed some giraffes in the distance.* (With inversion.)
This drought is not only severe, it is also unexpected. (Without inversion.)
*Not only **is this drought** severe, it is also unexpected.*

2   to emphasise degree (amount), using e.g. *so, such, much, many, more, most, little*:
The antelope little realised that it was being eyed by a watchful lion. (Without inversion.)
*Little **did the antelope** realise that it was being eyed by a watchful lion.* (With inversion. This emphasises how little the antelope realised what was happening.)

3   in second and third conditionals, placing *were, had* or *should* before the subject:
***Were** the nature reserve to be closed, the local tourism industry would collapse.* (= If the nature reserve were to be closed, or was closed)
***Had** any photographers been present, they would have been delighted with the opportunities the animals presented.* (= If any photographers had been present)
***Should** visitors visit this part of the rainforest, they must keep to the paths.*
(=If visitors [should] visit this part of the rainforest, they must keep to the paths.)

4   if we put adverbs of time or place, such as *here, there, out, in, then, now*, at the beginning of the sentence for emphasis:
***Here comes** a herd of elephants.*

Unit 8 Relative clauses

Defining relative clauses

Defining relative clauses are used to give information that is essential for identifying exactly what a noun refers to:
*The hotel **where Kate had a temporary job last summer** has just closed down.* (This gives essential information, defining which hotel the speaker means.)
*The restaurant offers work experience to people **who are studying catering**.* (This gives essential information, defining which people the speaker means.)

The relative pronouns used in defining relative clauses are: *which* or *that* (for things); *who* or *that* (for people); *where* (for places); *when* (for times); *whose* (to indicate possession, usually by people):
*There are times **when** my job becomes very stressful.*
*I enjoy working with people **who / that** are friendly.*
*I'd like to work with people **whose** sense of humour is similar to my own.*

If the relative pronoun is the object in the defining relative clause it can be omitted:

> The office **(that / which) he works in** gets very hot in the summer. (The office gets hot in the summer. He works **in the office**.)

In more formal English, prepositions can be moved from the end of the relative clause to before the relative pronoun. In these cases, only the relative pronouns *which* (for things) and *whom* (for people) can be used:

> The office **in which he works** gets very hot in the summer.
>
> The manager **to whom he reports** is very demanding. (This is a formal alternative to *The manager (who / that) he reports to is very demanding.*)

What is a pronoun meaning *the thing(s) that / which*. It isn't used to refer to people. Unlike relative pronouns, it doesn't follow a noun. If it is the subject of a clause, the verb is always singular:

> **What I enjoy most about going shopping** is chatting to people and finding bargains. (*what* introduces the subject of the sentence, i.e. The two things that I enjoy most about going shopping.)
>
> You'd better explain **what you mean**. (*what* introduces the direct object of the sentence.)
>
> The trainer devoted too little time to **what the trainees regarded as essential**. (*what* introduces something that follows a preposition.)
>
> This is **what I want to do for the rest of my life**. (*what* introduces the complement of the sentence.)

Non-defining relative clauses

Non-defining relative clauses are used to give extra information. This type of relative clause is usually separated from the main clause with commas. If the clause is omitted, it is still clear what exactly the noun refers to. This is not the case with defining relative clauses:

> Her brother who lives in Spain is a doctor. (Defining: she has more than one brother, but only one who lives in Spain.)
>
> Her brother, who lives in Spain, is a doctor. (Non-defining: she has only one brother, so 'who lives in Spain' is extra information. *Her brother* is enough to identify the person.)

We cannot use *that* or *what* in non-defining relative clauses.

The relative pronoun cannot be omitted from non-defining relative clauses:

> ~~Jill's job, **she really enjoys**, offers plenty of scope for promotion.~~
>
> Jill's job, **which she really enjoys**, offers plenty of scope for promotion. √

As in defining clauses, a preposition can come before the pronoun of a non-defining relative clause:

> I may be invited for a job interview, **in which case** I'll need to take a day off work.

The relative pronoun can follow a quantifier or noun, together with a preposition. This tends to occur in non-defining relative clauses, and in more formal language:

> She has two brothers, **both of whom** studied business.
>
> There are over a hundred applicants for the job, **most of whom** have had a great deal of work experience.
>
> The new film studies course, **an outline of which** is available on the college website, is attracting a large number of applicants.

Other uses

In both defining and non-defining relative clauses, *whose* generally refers to people rather than to things:

> The physicist **whose work won a Nobel prize** has since left the university.

The book, **whose theoretical basis is unreliable**, has been severely criticised. (This is a less common structure than the following, without *whose*.)

> This book, **which is based on an unreliable theory**, has been severely criticised.

Why and *that* can be used as a relative pronoun after *reason*:

> The reason **(why / that) there are so many students in the class** is that the lecturer is very well-known.

We can use *why* without *reason* as in the following example:

> Most graduates find jobs soon after leaving, which is (the reason) **why I applied to this university**.

Some relative clauses can be reduced by omitting the relative pronoun and auxiliary verb(s) and leaving the present or past participle. The auxiliary verb *be* can be omitted from a continuous tense, leaving the present participle (*-ing*):

> There were over fifty students **(who were) waiting for the lecturer to arrive**.
>
> Most people **(who / that are) hoping to meet the popular biologist will be disappointed**.

Similarly, if the relative clause is in the passive, the relative pronoun and auxiliary verb(s) can be omitted:

Several of the courses **(which / that are) offered by the college** have a very good reputation.

Unit 9 Modal verbs

There are many functions of modal verbs and some of the most common are listed here.

Ability

To express ability in the present, we use *can* or *be able to*:

*This apparatus **can** detect earth tremors. (A permanent characteristic.)*

*This apparatus **is able to** detect earth tremors. (A permanent characteristic.)*

*Julia **can** watch the programme tomorrow evening. (A single occasion.)*

*Julia **is able to** watch the programme tomorrow evening. (A single occasion.)*

For general ability in the past (i.e. continuing over a period of time), we use *could* or *be able to*:

*We **couldn't do / weren't able to do** many science experiments at school because we didn't have much equipment.*

*A lot of chemicals that you **could buy / were able to buy** in shops in the past are now on restricted sale.*

To express ability on one specific occasion in the past, we use *be able to*, not *could*:

*In the end, the college **was able to** raise enough money to buy new science equipment.*

Possibility and impossibility

To express possibility, we normally use *may*, *might* or *could*:

*This new TV programme about astronomy **may / might** be interesting. (**may** tends to express more confidence that it will happen than **might** does)*

*TV companies **could** make more of an effort to publicise their science programmes. (It is possible in theory, but TV companies haven't said anything about doing it.)*

To express past possibility, we use *could have*, *may have* or *might have*:

*The programme **could have** included more explanation of atoms. (It didn't.)*

*The presenter **may have / might have** forgotten that most viewers know very little about physics. (The speaker is speculating – he doesn't know if it happened.)*

To express an event that is impossible in the present, we use *can't*:

*I **can't** use my smartphone because the battery is flat.*

To express an event that is impossible in the past, we use *couldn't have*:

*The psychologist **couldn't have** won the prize without the work done by her team.*

Certainty and logical deduction

To express certainty because we have evidence, we use *must*:

*She goes abroad on holiday several times a year, so she **must** have a good income.*

To express certainty something is not the case, we use *can't*:

*This chemical reaction shows there **can't** be oxygen present.*

To express certainty about the past, we use *must have*:

*The audience **must have** thought the speaker had forgotten to bring his notes.*

To express certainty that something was *not* the case in the past, we use *can't have*:

*She **can't have** left her phone in the cinema – she made a call after the film.*

Obligation

To express obligation in the present, we often use *must* when the obligation comes from the speaker:

*You **must** all wash your hands thoroughly after working with chemicals. (The speaker is giving an order, or imposing an obligation.)*

When the obligation comes from elsewhere, we often use *have to*, or informally *have got to*:

*You **have to / 've got to** register in advance if you want to attend the lecture. (The speaker is reporting an order or obligation imposed by someone else.)*

*John **has to / 's got to** finish his homework before his parents allow him to go out.*

No obligation

To express a lack of obligation to do something, we normally use *don't have to* or *don't need to*:

*Pandas **don't have to / don't need to** move fast because they aren't attacked by other animals. (This is a factual lack of obligation.)*

*You **don't have to / don't need to** carry out any more experiments if you don't want to. (The lack of obligation could come from the speaker, from someone else, or from circumstances.)*

To show the lack of obligation is the speaker's decision, we use *needn't*:

*You **needn't** carry out any more experiments if you don't want to. (The lack of obligation could come from the speaker.)*

To show something was unnecessary in the past, and may or may not have happened, we use *didn't need to*:

*Sue **didn't need to** analyse the data because that had already been done. (It was clear at the time that it was unnecessary to analyse the data, implying that she probably didn't analyse it.)*

To express that something that happened was unnecessary, we use *needn't have*:

> Sue **needn't have** analysed the data because that had already been done. (She analysed the data, but it later became clear that it was unnecessary.)

Permission

To ask whether something is allowed, we use *can*, *could* or *may*. *Can* is informal, and *may* is formal:

> **Can / Could / May** I give my presentation first, please?

To express permission, we use *can* or *may* (which is formal):

> You **can / may** watch the student presentations as long as you don't interrupt.

To show something that was permitted as a general rule in the past, we use *could* or *be allowed to*:

> When I was a child, I **could / was allowed to** stay up late to watch educational programmes on TV.

To show something that was permitted on a particular occasion in the past, we use *be allowed to* not *could*:

> The children **were allowed to** stay up late last night to watch a TV programme about electronics.

To show something is not allowed, we use *can't* or *mustn't*:

> You **can't / mustn't** go into the main hall because there's an exam going on.

To show something was not allowed in the past, we use *couldn't*:

> When I was a child, I **couldn't** stay up late to watch TV, even to see educational programmes.

Recommendations

To make a recommendation, we often use *should / shouldn't* or, less often, *ought to / ought not to*:

> You **should / ought to** read this book if you want to really understand the subject.
> You **shouldn't / ought not to** let other people's phone conversations distract you.

The past forms are *should have / shouldn't have* and, less often, *ought to have / ought not to have*:

> The journalist **should have / ought to have** explained all the technical terms.
> The journalist **shouldn't have / oughtn't to have** assumed everyone was familiar with the technical terms.

Unit 10 Wishes and regrets

To talk about a present situation which we would like to change, we use *wish* or *if only* + past simple:

> Joanna **wishes** she **had** more time for going to concerts. (This is Joanna's wish.)
> If only Joanna **didn't work** so hard. (This is the speaker's wish.)
> I **wish** I **was / were** better at maths.

To express regret about a past situation, we can use *wish* or *if only* + past perfect:

> I **wish / If only I'd** been more self-confident when I was a teenager. (but I wasn't)

To express annoyance, we use *wish* or *if only* + *would*:

> I **wish / If only** people **would** stop saying I'm introverted. (It is annoying that people say that about me.)

To talk about something which we would like to happen in the future, we use *wish* or *if only* + subject + *could* + infinitive:

> I **wish I could go** to the theatre with you tomorrow. (I would like to go. This usually implies that I can't go.)
> If only I could go to the theatre with you tomorrow. (I feel very strongly that I would like to go. This implies that I can't go.)

To express a preference now, we use *would rather* + past simple if the subject of *would rather* is different from the subject of the following clause:

> I'd rather you didn't open the present just yet. (I is the subject of *would*; *you* is the subject of the following clause.)

When the two subjects are the same, the infinitive without *to* is used:

> Jake would rather **stay** at home.

To express a preference now about the past where the subjects are different, we use *would rather* + past perfect:

> Stephen **would rather** you **hadn't borrowed** his bike.

When the two subjects are the same, we use the perfect infinitive without *to* (*have done*):

> Zoe started work when she left school. She **would rather have gone** to university.

It's (about / high) time + past simple means that the speaker wants something to happen:

> It's **about time she realised** how narrow-minded she's being.
> It's **high time you made** up your mind about what career you want.

We cannot use *wish* + *would* + infinitive if the subject of *wish* is the same as the subject of would:

> ~~Kate wishes she would have her novel published.~~
> Kate wishes she could have her novel published. √

WRITING GUIDE

This is a guide to how to approach the Writing in *Cambridge English: Advanced*. It suggests some ways to prepare for it, and what you should bear in mind during the exam. You should refer to the 'During the exam' checklist as you work through the questions and model answers in the guide.

Before the exam

- In Writing you must answer Part 1, where there is no choice, and you must choose one of the three questions in Part 2. The same number of marks are available for both parts, so you should spend 45 minutes on each of your two answers.

- Work out how many lines of the answer sheet you need for 240 words in your handwriting. Then in the exam you can count the lines, which is much quicker than counting the words. The word limit of 220–260 should be one or two lines more or less than you need for 240 words.

- Time your writing, so that you know roughly how long it takes you to write 240 words. Once you've planned your answer, writing it will probably take around 20 minutes: this means there is plenty of time for planning and improving.

- Practise writing answers to *Cambridge English: Advanced* questions, spending no more than 45 minutes on each, including time for planning, writing and improving.

- Make sure you have answered the question fully, and that everything you have written is relevant.

- Get used to writing without dictionaries and computer spelling checks, as you can't use them in the exam.

- Keep a record of useful vocabulary and grammatical structures that you come across, including linking expressions, words that you might misspell, formal and informal synonyms, words used in connection with particular topics, and so on.

- Read a wide range of material in English. This will help you improve your own writing.

During the exam

- Read all the questions before you start work on either task. You do not have to write the Part 1 task first.
- Plan the amount of time you're going to spend on each task, dividing it into time for planning, writing and improving. You should spend a total of about 45 minutes on each task.

Planning

- Underline key words in the questions that will remind you what you need to write about. Then make a plan, just writing a few words or phrases for each point, and checking that they are in a logical order.
- Keep referring back to the question, to make sure that everything in your plan is relevant, and that your answer includes everything you are asked to do.

Writing

- Write your answer, making sure it is clear to the intended reader, and written in a style that is suitably formal or informal for that person.
- Try to use a wide variety of vocabulary and grammatical structures. Where appropriate, try to use synonyms rather than using the same word twice.
- Write full, grammatically correct sentences with good linking expressions, using a wide range of language, and avoiding spelling or punctuation errors.
- You should aim to write in either British or American English and not a mixture, particularly with regard to spelling.
- Estimate the length of your text, without wasting time counting every word.
- Don't waste time trying to remember a particular word: it's usually quicker to work out an alternative way of expressing the idea, perhaps by using a clause or sentence to explain what you mean.

Improving

- Read the question again, then read your answer, trying to imagine that you are the intended reader. Check that everything is clear.
- You may find it helpful to write *both* your answers before improving them: that way, you will read your answer with fresh eyes, and are more likely to see ways of making it better.

- Draw a line through anything that you don't want the examiners to read, and use letters, numbers or symbols like (A), (1) or * to show where something new should be read. If necessary, write notes for the examiners, e.g. 'Please read the third paragraph before the second.'
- After improving the content of your answer, read it again to check for 'spoilers', particularly grammar, spelling or punctuation mistakes. These can cost you marks if they make it difficult to understand what you mean.

Remember

- There are some blank pages at the back of the answer sheet, which you can use for your plans. Draw a line through these when you have finished as they are not part of the answer you want the examiners to read.
- If you use the blank pages for part of your final answer, make sure the examiners can see what to read, for example, you could write 'continued at (A)' and put (A) in the appropriate place on the blank pages.
- The examiners need to be able to read what you have written, so write as clearly as possible. It is best not to write entirely in capital letters.
- Your answers will be marked on how well they are written, not on whether the examiners agree with you.

Part 1

What to expect in Part 1

- Part 1 tests your ability to write an essay, developing and supporting an argument on a given topic, in 220–260 words.
- You are given a set of notes on the topic, including three bullet points. You must select two of the bullet points, and base your essay on those two points only.
- You will be asked to explain which of the two points is more important in a particular way, and to give reasons for your opinion.
- You are also given three short opinions related to the bullet points. You can use these to help develop your essay, if you want to, but you should do so **in your own words**, as far as possible.
- You should spend a total of about 45 minutes on the task, including time to plan and improve it.
- You need to organise your essay into paragraphs, with an appropriate beginning and ending.
- You should develop your essay by giving reasons for the opinions you express.
- Your essay should have a positive effect on the reader, be well organised with one part leading clearly to the next, and have a layout that makes it easy to read – particularly by being divided into paragraphs.
- You must write in a neutral to formal style.

How to do Part 1

- Read all the instructions and notes carefully. Underline the key words. Think about all three bullet points, and decide which two of them you prefer to write about.
- Make brief notes for: an introduction, each of the bullet points, and your conclusion.
- Your introduction could explain why the topic is important, for example, and refer to how the two bullet points relate to the topic.
- For each of the two chosen bullet points, you might find it useful to divide your notes into 'for' and 'against'. Make notes on your opinion, and your reasons for holding that opinion. You might also make notes on why other people might disagree with you.
- Decide whether you want to refer to any of the opinions included in the task. If so, make a note under the appropriate heading.
- Your conclusion should answer the question about which bullet point is more important.

Practice task and model answer

1 Read the Part 1 task below and answer the questions.

  1 What is the background situation?
  2 What is the topic of the essay?
  3 Who will read it?

You have attended a panel discussion on ways in which the needs of an ageing population can be met. You have made the notes below.

> **Ways in which the needs of an ageing population can be met**
> - more residential care homes
> - more jobs available for elderly people
> - more entertainment

> **Some opinions expressed in the discussion:**
> "I'd rather get help in my own home than move into a care home."
> "Work gives people a way of organising their day."
> "Too many forms of entertainment are intended for young people."

Write an essay for your tutor discussing **two** of the ways in your notes. You should explain **which way you think is more important giving reasons** to support your opinion.

You may, if you wish, make use of the opinions expressed in the discussion, but you should use your own words as far as possible.

2 Read this model essay and answer the questions.

  1 What style is the essay written in? Give three examples that show this.
  2 How has the writer organised the essay?
  3 In the writer's opinion, which way is more important?

> **Introduction, giving the background – why the population is ageing – and introducing areas where the elderly might have specific needs**

As medicine develops, life expectancy rises, increasing the proportion of the population over the age of 65. This presents numerous challenges for society as a whole, in areas ranging from healthcare to transport, and no country has fully come to grips with the issues involved.

Many more people survive strokes, heart attacks and other diseases than in the past, but they may suffer from impaired health and require assistance in some form. One solution is residential care homes, with trained support available round the clock. A major drawback, however, is the shortage of affordable places. Despite the high cost, governments should provide more homes, and, if necessary,

> **Reason**

subsidise the residents. Without this intervention, moving to a home would be out of reach of many people, who risk ending up without the support they need.

> **Good linking expression (In connection) indicating new topic**

In connection with the question of work, for many elderly people retirement brings empty days to fill, without the income required to pass the time enjoyably. Having a job can provide a structure that might once have seemed very

> **Good words as an alternative way of expressing second opinion**

demanding, but is now missed. Some people would rather work, perhaps from home, and perhaps part-time. Such activity could be organised at a local or even national level, with employers offering tasks that are suitable for retired people.

> **Conclusion and writer's opinion, with reason**

Much could be done to meet the needs of an ageing population, and it is hard to prioritise just one area. Nevertheless, I believe that having an adequate number of places in residential care homes to meet demand is probably the most important, as health is a fundamental need.

> **Linking word (nevertheless)**

Part 2

What to expect in Part 2

- Part 2 tests your ability to write one of the following texts in 220–260 words: **a formal or informal letter, a report, a proposal, a review**.
- You choose one task from three possible questions.
- Questions are based on a variety of topics, such as work, social issues, the environment, health, education and travel.
- For all Part 2 tasks you are given a context, a purpose for writing and an intended reader. The task may include a short text, such as a letter, notice or advertisement, plus instructions.
- Remember you have about 45 minutes to complete the task, including time to plan and improve it.
- To complete the task in full, you must deal with every element of the question.
- Remember that your aim, as in Part 1, is to communicate effectively with the person or organisation specified in the question. You need to make sure they can follow your line of argument and that you have written it in the correct tone.
- Your answer needs to be well organised, with one part leading clearly to the next, and to have a layout that makes it easy to read.
- Aim to demonstrate that you have a wide knowledge of English grammar and vocabulary, and to make sure your grammar, spelling and punctuation are correct – mistakes in any of these areas can cause communication difficulties.
- You need to organise your text into paragraphs, with an appropriate beginning and ending.
- You should develop your text, particularly by giving reasons for your opinions.

How to do Part 2

- Look quickly through questions 2–4 and decide which of them you think you can do best. If you don't fully understand a question (for example, if you don't understand to *sponsor* in the report question below), it's best not to answer that one.
- Study the task and highlight the points you must deal with. Think about the intended reader and therefore how formally you need to write.
- Make some notes on what to include. Then reread the question and your notes, and cross out any that aren't relevant to the question.
- Plan the structure of your answer, using a heading for each paragraph, including an introduction, your main topics, and a conclusion. Put your best ideas under paragraph headings. For a report or proposal you should use headings in your text, but not for letters or reviews.
- Add a few important words and phrases to your plan, but don't waste time writing complete sentences.
- Then reread the question, and write your answer, using your plan. If you move away from the plan, make absolutely sure that you are still answering the question.
- Remember to demonstrate your command of a wide range of English.

Letter

What to expect in a Part 2 letter

- You may need to write to, for example, the editor of a newspaper or magazine, the director of a company, the principal of a college or an English-speaking friend.
- Make sure you write in an appropriate style. To a friend you should write informally; to the other people mentioned above, write in a more formal style.
- A letter question may ask you to comment on something that has happened, give advice, express your feelings about something, describe your own or your company's needs, persuade, request, answer questions, etc.

How to do a Part 2 letter

- Plan your letter in paragraphs, and include an appropriate beginning and ending.
- Do not include any addresses.
- Make sure you deal with all the points that are specified.
- Begin your letter with the reader's name if you know it, e.g. *Dear Susie* to a friend or *Dear Ms Gerrard* to somebody you don't know personally. In the latter case, end your letter *Yours sincerely. Ms* is used when writing to a woman if you don't know whether or not she is married.
- If you don't know the reader's name, begin your letter *Dear Sir or Madam* when writing to an organisation and you don't know who the specific reader is going to be. In these cases, end with *Yours faithfully*.
- You shouldn't start a letter *Dear friend* or use job titles, such as *Dear Manager*.
- Make sure you use a range of expressions.
- Make sure the purpose of your letter is clear.

Practice task and model answer

1 Read the Part 2 task below and answer the questions.

1 Who must you write to?
2 What will be the main topic of your reply?
3 What requirements are there in the task?

You have received a letter from an English friend.

> I'm doing a project at college about how people's lives have changed over the last few decades in different countries. Can you tell me about the situation in your country? I'd like to hear about improvements and also about anything that's worse now.

Write your **letter** in reply. You do not need to include postal addresses.

---

2 Read the sample letter written by Mischa and answer the questions.

1 How appropriate is the style that Mischa has written in? Give three examples as evidence of this.
2 Is the organisation of his letter correct?
3 Which paragraphs deal with the various requirements of the task?

Dear Marian

Great to hear from you. I hope you're well and enjoying your college course.

> Letters begin with social remarks before introducing any major topic.

Your project sounds very interesting. I've just had a chat with my grandparents, to find out how their way of life has changed during their lifetime, and a few things came up that you might like to hear about.

> Introduces the main topic in a positive way.

They said their standard of living is much higher now than it used to be, mainly because they have far more money to spend – even though they're pensioners. When they were much younger, and my grandfather went out to work, it was a struggle to cope on the money he earned, especially as they had several children to bring up.

> The writer is surprised that, as pensioners, his grandparents have more money to spend.

Now they can spend much more on leisure activities and holidays, so whereas they couldn't afford to go abroad on holiday until they were in their 50s, nowadays they go skiing in Switzerland or Italy every winter, and in the summer they like to go on a river cruise in another country, too.

> Linking word (*whereas*) to introduce a contrast

The biggest change, they say, is in the amount of freedom that they have. As kids, they were under pressure from their families and everyone they knew had to do certain things and behave in certain ways, but now there's much greater tolerance of different ways of living.

> Informal vocabulary

On the other hand, they feel that people don't stick together the way they used to – instead of everyone helping each other, people tend to be more self-centred.

> Good linking expression in new paragraph, to show change from improvement to something that is worse now

Well, I hope you can use this in your project, Marian.

All the best
Mischa

> Short paragraphs common in informal letters

Report

What to expect in a Part 2 report

- A report task normally requires you to provide information – factual or invented – about a situation in the present or past. You may also be asked to suggest a future course of action.
- The instructions make the situation clear, and also who you are writing to: this could be, for example, a college tutor, a manager at work, or members of a club.

How to do a Part 2 report

- As with any question that you choose in Part 2, make sure you can quickly think of some relevant ideas to write about, possibly including any experience you or someone you know may have had.
- Make sure you write in an appropriate style: for a report this is usually neutral or formal.
- Plan your report in a logical order, using headings. The headings will depend on the precise situation, but the first might be *Background* or *Introduction* and the last might be *Recommendation*.

Practice task and model answer

1 Read the Part 2 task below and answer the questions.

1 What is the report about?
2 Who is the intended reader of your report?
3 What three things must you write about?

> Six months ago, your company started to sponsor a local sports club and your manager has asked you to write a progress report.
>
> Your report should explain why your company chose to sponsor that sports club, describe the form that the sponsorship takes, and suggest with reasons why it should or should not continue.
>
> Write your **report**.

2 Read this model report and answer the questions.

1 How formal is the report? Give three examples of this style.
2 Which heading matches each part of the instructions?
3 What recommendation is made?

Report on sponsorship of youth football team — [Title]

Introduction

The purpose of this report is to assess the company's sponsorship of the local youth football team.

Gives the purpose of the report, in different words from the instructions.

Reasons for sponsorship

Section headings

The company received negative publicity when a chemical leakage from the factory polluted the river. It was therefore decided that efforts should be made to improve the company's image locally. The town's youth football team was chosen as it was struggling financially. It was felt that helping the club would provide very positive publicity for the company.

Explains why the company decided to start sponsorship, and why it chose the football team.

Details of sponsorship

The company offered to meet the football club's expenses in full, initially for two years. Sponsorship covers the cost of hiring the council-owned football pitch that the club uses. Previously the club could only afford to hire the pitch for three hours once a week; the company has doubled this to two three-hour sessions each week.

Gives details of the form the sponsorship takes.

Shows how the club benefits from being sponsored.

The company has also agreed to pay for a new football kit for club members, which should be available before the start of the next football season.

Recommendation

Some letters in local newspapers suggest that the company's motives for sponsoring the team were suspect. However, this is outweighed by a considerable amount of positive publicity, as the youth football club is very popular in the town and its financial struggles were a cause of concern. For this reason, and because the sponsorship has raised the company's profile and greatly improved its image locally, I strongly recommend that we continue.

Considers both negative and positive effects.

Reports usually (but not always) include a recommendation about future action.

Proposal

What to expect in a Part 2 proposal

- The proposal task tests your ability to write persuasively. It focuses on a future action, requiring you to make one or more recommendations and to give reasons for making them.
- The instructions include a description of a situation.
- You may be asked to write for a manager, a tutor, or a group of people such as members of the same club.
- The main difference between a report and a proposal is that a report focuses on the present or past, possibly ending with a recommendation for the future, while a proposal focuses on future action, probably with information about the present or past that makes the recommended action necessary.

How to do a Part 2 proposal

- Before choosing a proposal question, be sure you can think of enough information about the topic to write a proposal. What you propose should seem reasonable, but remember your proposal is marked on the quality of your English, not on the quality of your ideas.
- Decide what style to use, depending on who the intended reader is. A proposal is usually written in a neutral or formal style.
- Note any knowledge or personal experience you can mention, and include this in your plan.
- Plan your proposal in a logical order, using headings. The headings will depend on the precise situation, but the first might be *Background* or *Introduction* and you might also need *Present situation* and *Recommendations*.

Practice task and model answer

1 Read the Part 2 task and answer the questions.

>   1   What is the topic of the proposal?
>   2   Who will read your proposal?
>   3   What two things do you have to do?

> You are studying at a university in the UK and see this notice on the website of the town council.
>
> > The town council is concerned that there are very few opportunities for foreign university students in the town to meet local residents. It has allocated a sum of money to be spent on improving contact.
> >
> > The council invites anyone interested to send a proposal outlining problems with the present situation and suggesting how it could be improved. The council will consider all proposals before making a decision.
>
> Write your **proposal.**

2 Read this model proposal and answer the questions.

1 What style is the proposal written in? Give three examples that show this.
2 Which headings correspond to which parts of the instructions?
3 What recommendation is made?

Improving contact between local residents and foreign students

Background

Since the foundation of the university five years ago, the number of foreign students has been growing year on year. There are now in the region of 500. Many live on campus, but a large number live in the town, mostly in rented accommodation which they tend to share with other foreign students.

> Some factual information that is relevant to the task.

Present situation

Within the university, students from all countries seem to be fully integrated. In the town, however, there is little social contact between foreign students and local residents.

> Use of linking word

Recommendation

My proposal is to run a course of cookery lessons, one evening a week throughout the academic year, with students from various countries, as well as local people, giving instruction in how to prepare dishes from their country or region.

> Presents the main points before going on to the justification and details.

Food is a shared interest of most people, and there is evidence that such classes create a friendly, sociable atmosphere. I suggest that each week, a group of people from a particular country are responsible for teaching and for helping the participants. This would increase the opportunities for interaction, compared with having only one trainer. The course should be held in a suitable venue that is accessible for both local people and students living on campus, such as the domestic science room in the secondary school.

> A justification for the proposal – not just the writer's opinion.

> Explains how the proposal cloud be implemented.

Support for proposal

I have discussed my proposal with a number of foreign students, and most of them are very enthusiastic about it as a way of broadening knowledge of their own culture, and of meeting local people.

> Shows backing for the writer's proposal – this makes it more convincing than if it is just one person's opinion.

Review

What to expect in a Part 2 review

- In a review you are normally asked to describe something you have experienced, e.g. a film, a visit to a tourist attraction or restaurant, a book, etc., and to give your opinion of it. You are asked to consider specific aspects of what you are reviewing.
- You might also be asked whether you would recommend it to other people.
- The question specifies where the review is to be published, for example, an English-language newspaper, magazine or website.
- The target reader is made clear, so you should write in an appropriate style and include appropriate information.

How to do a Part 2 review

- Make sure you read a wide range of reviews online, in newspapers and in magazines before the exam.
- Make notes of ways to express reservations, and how to move from positive to negative comments, or vice versa.
- Before starting to write a review, decide whether the overall impression you want to give is positive, negative or mixed. Keep this in mind, and make sure it is clear to the reader.
- Think about your experience, or simply use your imagination: you can invent the film, book, etc. that you write about.
- Think about your readers and what they will be interested in being told.
- Make sure the level of formality is appropriate for the people who will read your review.
- Make notes, and put them in a logical order using headings for your own use: reviews do not normally include headings.

Practice task and model answer

1 Read the Part 2 task and answer the questions.

1 What is being reviewed?
2 Where will the review be published and who are the intended readers?
3 What two things do you have to do as part of your review?

> You see the announcement below in a local magazine called *Eating out*.
>
> > **Improving the eating out experience**
> >
> > We have numerous restaurants in this area, so it can be hard for people to decide where to eat. That's why we want to publish reviews of restaurants. We're particularly interested in why you had certain expectations of a restaurant, and whether your experience in the restaurant was better – or worse – than you had expected.
> >
> > Send us your review of a restaurant where you've eaten, explain what your expectations were, and give your reasons for your opinions.

2 Read this model review. In which paragraph(s) can you find the following?

1 a summary of the writer's intentions regarding returning to the restaurant
2 a description of the writer's expectations of the evening
3 an explanation of why the writer had certain expectations

Review of 'Lanterns'

'Lanterns' is the most expensive restaurant in this area and its advertising stresses its upmarket characteristics, with photos of well-dressed guests, candles and linen napkins on the tables, for instance. You can hardly blame me for expecting everything to be first class: the venue itself, the food and of course the service.

> *Introduces the restaurant, giving readers who don't know it a clear idea of what it is like.*

> *Addresses the reader directly, to make them feel involved.*

I took my parents to 'Lanterns' to celebrate their golden wedding anniversary, intending it to be not just a meal, but a special occasion that we would all look back on with pleasure for years to come.

> *The first person 'I' emphasises the personal nature of the review. Makes it less formal.*

Unfortunately, our evening was nothing of the sort. Admittedly the atmosphere of the restaurant seemed very welcoming when we arrived, as was the waiter who greeted us, but we stood waiting for several minutes before being shown to our table. And 'waiting' was the keynote of the evening: a long pause before we were given menus, and a long enough wait for each course to make us think somebody had been sent out to buy the ingredients.

> *Informal phrase*

> *Linking expression (Admittedly) to indicate that what follows contrasts with what is said in the previous sentence.*

The food itself was pleasant enough, but bland. I know not everyone wants salt in their food, but some pepper, herbs or spices wouldn't have gone amiss.

As I paid the extremely large bill, the waiter asked if we'd enjoyed the evening. I said the service had been slow, expecting an apology. Instead he tried to justify it, saying that most guests are not in a rush. Well, neither were we, but we still felt we'd been forced to stay considerably longer than we wanted to. 'Lanterns' certainly won't be seeing me again.

> *Informal word suitable for the personal tone of the review.*

SPEAKING GUIDE

This guide will help you prepare for the Speaking test in the *Cambridge English: Advanced* examination.

About the Speaking test

- The test lasts for 15 minutes for two candidates and 23 minutes for three.
- There are always two examiners. One talks to you and assesses your English; the other assesses your English without talking to you.
- You need to be able to answer questions, talk without interruption for a minute, and play an active role in discussion. You also need to be able to develop an argument systematically, explain why you agree or disagree with someone else's opinions, express shades of opinion and certainty, speculate, and so on.
- Your English is assessed on your performance throughout the test, on the following basis:
  - o the range of grammatical forms you use
  - o the range of appropriate vocabulary you use
  - o your ability to produce extended stretches of language with ease and with very little hesitation, while providing contributions that are relevant, coherent and varied, and using a wide range of linking words and phrases
  - o your pronunciation
  - o your interaction with the examiner and other candidate(s) and how you negotiate towards an outcome.

Before the Speaking test

- Familiarise yourself with all parts of the Speaking test, and think how you can best demonstrate your command of English.
- Listen to programmes in English on the television, radio or Internet. In talks, pay attention to how the speaker leads the listener through their argument, for example by using linking words and phrases. In discussions, notice how people interact with each other, how they express their opinion, concede a point, try to persuade, and so on.
- Keep a vocabulary book, where you write new words and phrases with explanations (in English) of the meaning, and examples showing how they are used in sentences.
- Also make lists of functional phrases and sentences, that is, what you can say to disagree politely, interrupt politely, explain again when the listener hasn't understood, paraphrase when you can't think of a particular word, and so on.

Part 1

What to expect in Part 1

- It is about two minutes long.
- The questions you are asked are intended to help you relax.
- They focus on you and aspects of your life, such as your work or studies, where you live, how you spend your free time, etc.

How to prepare for Part 1

- Don't learn complete sentences – be spontaneous!
- You might find it useful to make a list of questions about yourself, your work or studies, hopes and plans, or hobbies.
- Consider what you could say about various aspects of where you live.
- If you're in an English-speaking country, look for situations where you need to speak English, for example, join a club.
- Role-play situations with other students.

How to do Part 1

- Aim to answer each question in a couple of sentences – not with just a word or phrase. Think of the question as a starting point; for example, if you are asked where you live, you could name the place, say whether it is a city, town or village, then briefly describe it, and go on to say how you feel about living there.
- Make sure the other candidate and both the examiners can hear you. This is particularly important to remember if you normally speak quietly, or are nervous.
- Try to look and sound confident! Look at the examiner when he or she is speaking to you. Taking deep breaths may help you to relax.

Useful language for Part 1

Asking for repetition

Sorry. Would you mind repeating that, please?
I'm afraid I didn't quite get that.
Could I ask you to say that again, please?

Giving reasons and explanations

The reason I like it is ...
It may not be obvious, but the reason is ...
Let me just explain why.

Giving examples

One of the main attractions of the town is ...
The best example is probably ...

Developing a point

Let me expand on that.

Talking about possibilities

I haven't made up my mind yet, but I might ...
I'm thinking of ... , but I haven't decided yet.
One possibility that I'm considering is ...

Part 2

What to expect in Part 2

- It is about four minutes long.
- The examiner gives you three colour photos, and will ask you to choose *two* of them to compare, and then answer two questions.
- You can also read the questions which are printed on the same page.
- You need to speak in a coherent, organised way, using the two photos as a starting point for demonstrating your knowledge of grammar and vocabulary.
- To answer the questions, you will need to speculate, for example about how the people in the photographs feel, or the effects of their actions.
- You have one minute for this 'long turn'. Nobody will interrupt you while you are speaking.
- When you have finished, the examiner will ask the other candidate a question about your photos.
- Listen to the other candidate while they are speaking, as the examiner will then ask you a question about their photos. You have up to 30 seconds for your answer.

How to prepare for Part 2

- Look for images on the Internet by entering a word or phrase, such as 'happiness' or 'people enjoying music'. Then spend some time talking about them with a partner. Think about how to organise what you're going to say, for example: what the images have in common; what's different; why the people are in those situations; how they probably feel; what might happen next.
- Don't just describe the images, but speculate about feelings, what might have just happened, and so on. You should also compare the images.
- If possible, do this with a friend, so that you get ideas from each other about what you might say.
- Record and listen to yourself, to identify ways in which you can improve. So, for example, if you hesitate quite a lot, you should practise speaking some more, or if you mostly use simple sentences, try to use more complex structures.
- Ask people to listen to you speaking for a minute or two about two images, and ask them to comment and suggest ways of improving.
- Get used to how much you can say in a minute, by timing yourself while you are talking. If you find that you run out of things to say before a minute is up, stop and think about what else you could find to say about the images, then try again. If you speak for less than a minute in the test, you aren't giving yourself enough time to show how much English you know.
- Spend some time thinking about what you could say about two particular images, and try writing a talk about them. You should aim at about 150 words for a one-minute talk.

How to do Part 2

- Listen carefully to the two questions and read them in the booklet you are given showing the photos.
- Quickly decide which two photos you could find most to talk about, and make sure you only talk about those two.
- Start by saying which two pictures you intend to talk about.
- Make sure you answer the questions.
- Don't give a detailed description of the photos: your aim is to compare and contrast them, and to answer the questions in some depth.
- If you can't think of a particular word you need, you can refer to it in a different way. See *Useful language for Part 2*.
- Don't worry about making mistakes: you don't need to speak perfect English in order to do well. If you realise you've made a mistake, you can quickly correct yourself .
- When you answer the questions, don't simply give your opinion: it needs to be supported by reasons and examples.

Useful language for Part 2

Saying which pictures you're talking about

I'm going to compare the picture on the left with the one in the centre.
I've chosen the photograph that shows … and the one with …

Describing similarities

In certain respects the pictures are quite similar because …
What the two photos share is …
They're quite alike in that …
A common feature of both photos is …

Describing differences

What makes the two photos different is …
The biggest difference between them is …
What distinguishes the two pictures is …
While / Whereas the people in one photo seem to be … , in the other one people are …

Speculating

They might be …
It's just possible that they're …
I wouldn't be surprised if …
There's just a chance that they're …

Giving your opinion

In my opinion, …
I'd say that …
It seems to me …
My own feeling is that …
My own view is that …
If you ask me, …

Putting forward an opinion you don't agree with

Some people might think that … , but to me …
It's sometimes said that … , but …
Admittedly it might be argued that … . However, …

If you can't think of a particular word

I can't remember what it's called, but it's used when …
The word has just gone out of my head. It means something like …

Part 3

What to expect in Part 3

- It is about four minutes long.
- It is a discussion between you and the other candidate. The examiner will give you a task, and will then stay out of the discussion.
- There is no right or wrong answer, and you won't be penalised if you don't reach a decision.
- You need to be able to play an active role in an in-depth discussion, which includes developing an argument systematically, explaining why you agree or disagree with someone else's opinions, expressing shades of opinion and certainty, and so on.
- The examiner asks you and your partner to discuss some written stimuli, consisting of a question in a box, with brief descriptions of around five situations.
- You have 15 seconds to read the question and situations, then the examiner will ask you the question that is in the box. You have two minutes for your discussion.
- After two minutes, the examiner will ask you a different question about the stimuli, and you have a minute to discuss that question and make a decision.

How to prepare for Part 3

- Think of various situations that involve making a decision, for example, reasons for going to university in another country. Write down as many relevant factors as you can think of. This will help you to think quickly of points to make in the test.
- Record your discussion and listen to it, thinking about how you can improve the way you take part. Notice, for example, whether you dominate the conversation or take a passive role. In both cases you should aim to play a more equal part in the discussion.
- Make sure you carry out a range of functions, for example, asking for the other person's opinion, commenting on it, expressing an opinion persuasively, expressing degrees of certainty, etc.
- Make sure your discussion lasts for two minutes, so that you get used to speaking for the full time.

How to do Part 3

- Listen carefully to the instructions and use the 15 seconds to read and think about the written stimuli.
- When the examiner asks you the question, after 15 seconds, start straightaway. See *Useful language* below.
- Talk briefly about each situation, giving reasons for your opinions and for your responses to your partner's comments.
- Don't always agree with your partner. If you disagree, say so politely. If you agree, say so, but you could also mention what some other people might think. See *Useful language* below.
- If you have personal experience of the situations, you could mention that. If not, speculate about the situations. See *Useful language* in Part 2.
- Aim to talk about all the situations in the time available. From time to time, suggest moving on to the next situation. See *Useful language* below.
- After two minutes, the examiner will ask you a question requiring a decision. You won't be penalised if you don't have time to reach a decision.
- If the other candidate doesn't say much, encourage them by asking them what they think, or asking their reasons for holding their opinions. See *Useful language* below.
- If you feel the other candidate isn't giving you a chance to speak, you should interrupt them politely. See *Useful language* below.

Useful language for Part 3

Getting started
Shall we start with this one?
Let's make a start.
Would you like to kick off, or shall I?
That's quite an interesting question. What's your opinion?

Agreeing
That's just what I was thinking.
That's a very good point.
Absolutely.
You've got a point there.
That's exactly what I would have said.

Agreeing, but mentioning other people's opinions
I totally agree, but some people might say …
I'm with you on that, but it's sometimes claimed that …

Disagreeing and giving reasons
I'm not sure I agree. For one thing, … . And for another, …
I don't really see it quite that way. After all, …

Asking the other person to comment on your opinion
Would you go along with that?
Would you agree with that?
How do you feel about that?
What do you reckon?

Asking for reasons
Why do you say that?
Is there any particular reason why you think that?
Is that because … ?

Asking for clarification
I'm not sure I follow you.
What exactly do you mean?
Could you explain in a little more detail, please?

Clarifying
Sorry if I didn't explain it very well. What I meant was …
Let me put it another way.
That wasn't quite what I had in mind. I meant something like …

Interrupting politely
Could I just come in here?
Let me just add to what you're saying.
Sorry, but could I just say …

Managing the conversation
Shall we move on?
Let's go on to the next one.
What about this situation?

Reaching a decision
Which one do you think is the most important?
Do you think we've settled the question?
We've got very different opinions, so let's agree to differ.

Part 4

What to expect in Part 4

- It is about five minutes long.
- The examiner asks you spoken questions, and you discuss them with the other candidate.
- The questions are related to the topic in Part 3.
- You will need to express and justify opinions, agree or disagree, and speculate.
- The examiner may ask you to respond to an opinion the other candidate has expressed, so listen carefully to what they say.

How to prepare for Part 4

- With one or two other students, find topics for discussion, such as stories in the news, or events in your own or other people's lives.
- Brainstorm words and phrases that might be useful in relation to each topic. If you keep a vocabulary book, make lists, using the topics as headings. Remember to include examples of sentences containing the words and phrases.
- Ask each other WH-questions (Who? Where? When? How? Why?), as these lead to more detailed answers than yes/no questions.
- See also suggestions for preparing for Part 3.

How to do Part 4

- Listen carefully to the questions (you won't be able to read them).
- You should answer the questions in more depth and at greater length than in Part 1.
- If you don't have an opinion already, explore possibilities and speculate. See *Useful language* below. Don't just say *I don't know.*
- Respond to what the other candidate says. While they are speaking, you could agree briefly by saying *Exactly* or *That's true*. Respond at greater length when they finish speaking.
- Remember that the assessment is based on the quality of your English – not on your opinions or whether or not the examiner agrees with you.

Useful language for Part 4

What to say if you're not sure of the question
If I've understood the question correctly, ...
I may have got this completely wrong, but I think ...

What to say if you haven't formed an opinion
It isn't something I know much about, but ...
I've never really thought about it before, but ...

Exploring possibilities and speculating
I'm not sure, but perhaps ...
It's conceivable that ...
It strikes me that this might ...

Trying to change someone's opinion
But what about ...?
Maybe, but isn't it true that ...?
Though wouldn't you agree that ...?
Isn't it possible that ...?

Adding points
There's also the fact that ...
In addition, ...
We also shouldn't forget the fact / possibility that ...

WORDLIST

adj = adjective, adv = adverb, n = noun, v = verb,
pv = phrasal verb, prep = preposition, exp = expression
conj = conjunction

Unit 1

alarmed *adj* worried or frightened by something (8)

appalled *adj* very shocked and feeling great disapproval (8)

break *v* (*news*) If news or a story breaks, or if someone breaks it, it becomes known by the public for the first time. (12)

circulation *n* (*of newspaper*) the number of people that a newspaper or magazine is regularly sold to (11)

contrary to *adj + prep* opposite to what someone said or thought (14)

conversely *adv* in an opposite way (14)

cover *v* (*news story*) to report the news about a particular important event (11)

current affairs *n* political news about events happening now (10)

demography *n* The demography of an area is the number and characteristics of the people who live in an area, in relation to their age, sex, if they are married or not, etc. (10)

disgusted *adj* feeling extreme dislike or disapproval of something (8)

distressed *adj* upset or worried (8)

draft *v* to write down a document for the first time, including the main points but not all the details (11)

helpless *adj* unable to do anything to help yourself or anyone else (8)

hysterical *adj* unable to control your feelings or behaviour because you are extremely frightened, angry, excited, etc. (8)

imply *v* to communicate an idea or feeling without saying it directly (13)

infer *v* to form an opinion or guess that something is true because of the information that you have (13)

irritated *adj* annoyed (8)

overwhelmed *adj* feeling sudden strong emotion (8)

phenomenon *n* something that exists or happens, especially something unusual or interesting (11)

readership *n* the group of people who regularly read a particular newspaper, magazine, etc. (11)

revenue *n* the income that a government or company receives regularly (11)

run *v* (*publish*) to publish something in a newspaper or magazine (11)

source *n* (*of information*) someone or something that supplies information (12)

speechless *adj* unable to speak because you are so angry, shocked, surprised, etc. (8)

subscription *n* an amount of money that you pay regularly to receive a product or service or to be a member of an organisation (11)

tablet *n* (*computer*) a small, flat computer that is controlled by touching the screen or by using a special pen (11)

transition *n* a change from one form or type to another, or the process by which this happens (10)

unsafe *adj* not safe (8)

Unit 2

allude to *pv* to mention someone or something without talking about them directly (17)

applause *n* the sound of people clapping their hands repeatedly to show enjoyment or approval of something such as a performance or speech (20)

bilingual *adj* (*of a person*) able to use two languages equally well, or (*of a thing*) using or involving two languages (19)

chilly *adj* (*of weather, conditions in a room, or parts of the body*) cold (23)

discourse *n* a speech or piece of writing about a particular, usually serious, subject (17)

edible *adj* suitable or safe for eating (23)

enhanced *adj* improved (17)

ethically *adv* in a way that is morally right (17)

feast *n* a day on which a religious event or person is remembered and celebrated (20)

gathering *n* a party or a meeting when many people come together as a group (20)

hence *adv* that is the reason or explanation for something (17)

inevitably *adv* in a way that cannot be avoided (19)

itinerary *n* a detailed plan or route of a journey (20)

luxurious *adj* very comfortable and expensive (19)

mislead *v* to cause someone to believe something that is not true (19)

motivated *adj* If someone is motivated by a particular desire or belief, that desire or belief causes them to behave in the way that they do. (17)

negligible *adj* too slight or small in amount to be of importance (17)

outnumber *v* to be greater in number than someone or something (19)

overcrowded *adj* containing too many people or things (19)

participant *n* a person who takes part in or becomes involved in a particular activity (20)

procession *n* a line of people who are all walking or travelling in the same direction, especially in a formal way as part of a religious ceremony or public celebration (20)

redevelop *v* to change an area of a town by replacing old buildings, roads, etc. with new ones (19)

refreshed *adj* less hot or tired (19)

scenario *n* a description of possible actions or events (17)

symptomatic *adj* If something bad is symptomatic of something else, it is caused by the other thing and is proof that it exists. (17)

unspoilt *adj* not changed or damaged by people (19)

voluntary *adj* Voluntary work is done without being paid and usually involves helping people. (16)

whilst *conj* while (17)

workshop *n* a meeting of people to discuss and/or perform practical work in a subject or activity (23)

Unit 3

be inclined to *exp* to have an opinion about something, but not a strong opinion (29)

close-knit *adj* describes a group of people in which everyone helps and supports each other (24)

come up with *pv* to suggest or think of an idea or plan (27)

distant relative *n* someone in your family who is not closely related (24)

dysfunctional *adj* not behaving or working normally (24)

extended family *n* a family unit that includes grandmothers, grandfathers, aunts and uncles, etc. in addition to parents and children (24)

foster parent *n* a person who acts as the parent of someone else's child for a limited period, without becoming their legal parent (24)

keep a low profile *exp* to avoid attracting attention to yourself (28)

keep a straight face *exp* to manage to stop yourself from smiling or laughing (28)

keep an eye out for *exp* to watch carefully for someone or something to appear (28)

keep someone posted *exp* to make sure that someone always knows what is happening (28)

keep track of *exp* to continue to know about something (28)

keep your cool *exp* to stay calm (28)

keep your fingers crossed *exp* to hope that things will happen in the way that you want them to (28)

keep your word *exp* to do what you said you would (28)

lifelong *adj* lasting for the whole of a person's life (24)

lone parent *n* someone who has a child or children, but no partner living with them (24)

meet up *pv* to meet another person in order to do something together (27)

mutual *adj* (of two or more people or groups) feeling the same emotion, or doing the same thing to or for each other (24)

neutral *adj* (style) neither formal nor informal (30)

spring up *pv* (*appear*) to appear suddenly (27)

stable *adj* (relationship) not likely to change or end suddenly (24)

stand up to *pv* to defend yourself against a powerful person or organisation when they treat you unfairly (28)

to cap it all *exp* used when you mention something in addition to all the other (bad) things that have happened (31)

Unit 4

affluent *adj* having a lot of money or owning a lot of things (36)

auction *n* a usually public sale of goods or property, where people make higher and higher bids (=offers of money) for each thing, until the thing is sold to the person who will pay most (34)

back out *pv* to decide not to do something that you said you would do (33)

bail out *pv* to help a person or organisation that is in difficulty, usually by giving or lending them money (33)

bankrupt *adj* declared by law as unable to pay what you owe (36)

bid *n* an offer of a particular amount of money for something that is for sale (34)

break even *exp* to have no profit or loss at the end of a business activity (36)

by and large *exp* when everything about a situation is considered together (35)

deduct *v* to take away an amount or part from a total (34)

first and foremost *exp* more than anything else (35)

for a start *exp* first, or as the first in a set of things (35)

for good *exp* for ever (35)

for the time being *exp* a particular period of time for which something has been happening, or that is needed for something (35)

funds *n* (*plural*) money needed or available to spend on something (36)

gross *adj* (*before tax*) A gross amount of money has not had taxes or other costs taken from it. (36)

interest *n* (*money charged on loan*) money that is charged by a bank or other financial organisation for borrowing money (36)

let alone *exp* used after a negative statement to emphasise how unlikely a situation is because something much more likely has never happened (35)

make a loss *exp* to lose more money than you make (34)

make ends meet *exp* to have just enough money to pay for the things that you need (36)

other than *exp* in a negative sentence, used to mean 'except' (35)

overdrawn *adj* (*of a person*) having taken more money out of your bank account than the account contained, or (of a bank account) having had more money taken from it than was originally in it (36)

pay-as-you-go *adj* describes a system in which you pay for a service before you use it and you cannot use more than you have paid for (34)

procedure *n* a set of actions that is the official or accepted way of doing something (34)

prosperous *adj* successful, usually by earning a lot of money (36)

rip-off *n* (*informal*) something that is not worth what you pay for it (36)

splash out on *pv* to spend a lot of money on buying things, especially on things that are pleasant to have but that you do not need (33)

subject to *exp* likely to be affected by something (35)

transaction *n* an occasion when someone buys or sells something, or when money is exchanged or the activity of buying or selling something (34)

unaffordable *adj* too expensive for people to be able to buy or pay for (36)

well off *adj* rich (36)

with a view to doing something *exp* with the aim of doing something (35)

Unit 5

blister *n* a painful swelling on the skin that contains liquid, caused usually by continuous rubbing, especially on your foot, or by burning (42)

clinical *adj* describes medical work or teaching that relates to the examination and treatment of ill people (40)

comparable *adj* similar in size, amount, or quality to something else (44)

competence *n* the ability to do something well (44)

conscious *adj* (*awake*) awake, thinking, and knowing what is happening around you (40)

conventional wisdom *n* beliefs or opinions that have existed for a long time and that most people agree with (43)

disclocate *v* to force a bone suddenly out of its correct position (42)

first-rate *adj* extremely good (45)

fracture *v* If a bone fractures or is fractured, it breaks or cracks. (42)

infect *v* to pass a disease to a person, animal, or plant; If a place, wound, or substance is infected, it contains bacteria or other things that can cause disease. (40)

make a point of *exp* to always do something or to take particular care to do something (43)

needless to say *exp* as you would expect; added to, or used to introduce, a remark giving information that is expected and not surprising (43)

on the grounds that *exp* a reason for what you do or say, or for being allowed to say or do something (43)

paramedic *n* a person who is trained to do medical work, especially in an emergency, but who is not a doctor or nurse (41)

pointless *adj* Something that is pointless has no purpose and it is a waste of time doing it. (44)

relief *n* rest from something difficult (43)

skilful *adj* good at doing something, especially because you have practised doing it (44)

specific *adj* relating to one thing and not others; clear and exact (44)

sprain *v* to cause an injury to a joint (= place where two bones are connected) by a sudden movement (42)

statistical *adj* relating to statistics (44)

strike a balance *exp* If you strike a balance between two things, you accept parts of both things in order to satisfy some of the demands of both sides in an argument, rather than all the demands of just one side (43)

summarise *v* to express the most important facts or ideas in a short and clear form (44)

surgeon *n* a doctor who is specially trained to perform medical operations (40)

surgical *adj* connected with or used for medical operations (40)

swelling *n* a part of your body that has become bigger because of illness or injury (42)

take issue with *exp* to disagree with strongly (43)

take note of *exp* to give attention to something, especially because it is important (43)

Unit 6

acclaimed *adj* praised and approved of (48)

allocate *v* to give something to someone as their share of a total amount, for them to use in a particular way (51)

anticipate *v* to imagine or expect that something will happen (48)

appalling *adj* shocking and very bad (48)

assign *v* If you assign a time for a job or activity, you decide it will be done during that time. (51)

brutal *adj* cruel, violent, and completely without feelings (54)

distinctive *adj* Something that is distinctive is easy to recognise because it is different from other things. (48)

evaluate *v* to judge or calculate the quality, importance, amount, or value of something (51)

exhibit *n* an object that is shown to the public in a museum, etc. (51)

exposure *n* (*made public*) the fact of something bad that someone has done being made public (51)

far-fetched *adj* very unlikely to be true, and difficult to believe (54)

gloomy *adj* unhappy and without hope (54)

gripping *adj* describes something that is so interesting or exciting that it holds your attention completely (54)

hilarious *adj* extremely funny and causing a lot of laughter (48)

imaginative *adj* new, original, and clever; good at thinking of new, original, and clever ideas (48)

outdated *adj* old-fashioned and therefore not as good or as fashionable as something modern (51)

overrated *adj* If something or someone is overrated, they are considered to be better or more important than they really are. (48)

predictable *adj* happening or behaving in a way that you expect and not unusual or interesting (54)

pretentious *adj* trying to appear or sound more important or clever than you are, especially in matters of art and literature (54)

renovate *v* to repair and improve something, especially a building (51)

subtle *adj* achieved in a quiet way that does not attract attention to itself and is therefore good or clever (54)

tedious *adj* boring (48)

unconventional *adj* different from what is usual or from the way most people do things (48)

unconvincing *adj* If an explanation or story is unconvincing, it does not sound or seem true or real. (54)

uninspired *adj* not exciting or interesting (54)

urge *v* to strongly advise or try to persuade someone to do a particular thing (51)

utterly *adv* completely (48)

view *v* to look at or watch something (49)

Unit 7

a breath of fresh air *exp* someone or something that is new and different and makes everything seem more exciting (61)

a drop in the ocean *exp* a very small amount compared to the amount needed (61)

commuter *n* someone who regularly travels between work and home (58)

congestion *n* traffic on roads or in towns, making movement difficult (58)

consumption *n* the amount used (58)

designated *adj* officially having the stated purpose (57)

down to earth *exp* sensible and practical (61)

drought *n* a long period when there is little or no rain (56)

emission *n* an amount of gas, heat, light, etc. that is sent out (56)

exhaust fumes *n (plural)* the waste gas from an engine, especially a car's (58)

extinct *adj* not now existing (56)

fossil fuel *n* fuels, such as gas, coal and oil, that were formed underground from plant and animal remains millions of years ago (56)

gridlock *n* a situation where roads in a town become so blocked by cars that it is impossible for any traffic to move (58)

habitat *n* the natural environment in which an animal or plant usually lives (56)

ice cap *n* a thick layer of ice that permanently covers an area of land (56)

keep your head above water *exp* to just be able to manage, especially when you have financial difficulties (61)

legislation *n* a law or set of laws suggested by a government and made official by a parliament (63)

mysteriously *adv* in a way that is strange and cannot be understood (62)

occupancy *n* someone's use of a room, building or vehicle (58)

out of the blue *exp* If something happens out of the blue, it is completely unexpected. (61)

over the moon *exp* delighted about something (61)

play with fire *exp* to act in a way that is very dangerous and to take risks (61)

smog *n* a mixture of smoke, gases, and chemicals, especially in cities, that makes the atmosphere difficult to breathe and harmful for health (58)

tip of the iceberg *exp* a small, noticeable part of a problem, the total size of which is really much greater (61)

unsurprisingly *adv* in a way that does not make you feel surprised (62)

Unit 8

adopt a low profile *exp* to avoid attracting attention to yourself (65)

appoint *v* to choose someone officially for a job or responsibility (68)

be what counts *exp* to have most importance or value (65)

brim with *exp* If someone is brimming with a good quality or thing, they have a lot of it. (65)

come to a conclusion *exp* to decide what to think about something (65)

die down *pv* to gradually decrease (65)

dismiss *v (sack)* to remove someone from their job, especially because they have done something wrong (68)

enrol *v* to put yourself or someone else onto the official list of members of a course, college, or group (64)

fill a position *exp* to find someone to do a job (68)

get the drift *exp* to understand the general meaning of what someone is saying (65)

go round in circles *exp* to keep doing or talking about the same thing, without achieving anything (65)

hold down a job *exp* to manage to keep a job for a period of time (68)

lay off *pv* to stop employing someone, usually because there is no work for them to do (68)

let go *exp* (sack) to stop employing someone, usually because there is no work for them to do (68)

make redundant *exp* to stop employing someone, usually because there is no work for them to do (68)

open-ended *adj* An open-ended activity or situation does not have a planned ending, so it may develop in several ways. (65)

postgraduate *n* a student who has already got one degree and is studying at a university for a more advanced qualification (64)

prospectus *n* a document giving details of a college, school, or business and its activities (64)

recruit *v* to persuade someone to work for a company or become a new member of an organisation, especially the army (68)

scholarship *n* an amount of money given by a school, college, university, or other organisation to pay for the studies of a person with great ability but little money (64)

step down *pv* to leave an important job or position, especially to allow someone else to take your place (68)

syllabus *n* (a plan showing) the subjects or books to be studied in a particular course, especially a course that leads to an exam (64)

take a back seat *exp* to choose not to be in a position of responsibility in an organisation or activity (65)

the matter in hand *exp* the subject or situation being considered (65)

tutorial *n* a period of study with a tutor involving one student or a small group (64)

undergraduate *n* a student who is studying for their first degree at college or university (64)

biased *adj* showing an unreasonable like or dislike for a person based on personal opinions (76)

compatible *adj* able to exist, live together, or work successfully with something or someone else (76)

criteria *n (plural)* standards by which you judge, decide about, or deal with something (72)

deduction *n* the process of reaching a decision or answer by thinking about the known facts, or the decision that is reached (72)

deprived *adj* not having the things that are necessary for a pleasant life, such as enough money, food, or good living conditions (76)

dumb down *pv* to make something simpler and easier to understand, especially in order to make it more popular (74)

eligible *adj* having the necessary qualities or satisfying the necessary conditions (76)

equivalent *adj* having the same amount, value, purpose, qualities, etc. as something else (76)

hostile (to) *adj* unfriendly and not liking or agreeing with something (76)

hypothesis *n* an idea or explanation for something that is based on known facts but has not yet been proved (72)

ignorant *adj* not having enough knowledge, understanding, or information about something (76)

in a sense *exp* thinking about something in one way, but not in every way (75)

inadequate *adj* not good enough or too low in quality (76)

be a matter of *exp* If something is a matter of doing a particular thing, that is what you need to do in order to achieve it. (75)

journal *n* a serious magazine or newspaper that is published regularly about a particular subject (74)

knowledgeable *adj* knowing a lot (76)

notorious *adj* famous for something bad (76)

prejudiced *adj* showing an unreasonable dislike for something or someone (76)

principle *n* a basic idea or rule that explains or controls how something happens or works (72)

protective (toward) *adj* wanting to protect someone from criticism, hurt, danger, etc. because you like them very much (76)

renowned *adj* famous for something (76)

restricted *adj* limited, especially by official rules, laws, etc. (76)

sceptical *adj* doubting that something is true or useful (76)

significance *n* important because it affects other things (72)

superior *adj* better than average or better than other people or things of the same type (76)

take a dim view *exp* to disapprove of something (74)

the former *exp* the first of two people, things, or groups previously mentioned (74)

the odd *exp* the occasional (75)

the status quo *exp* the present situation (75)

variable *n* a number, amount, or situation that can change (72)

Unit 10

antisocial *adj* often avoiding spending time with other people (84)

brush up on *pv* to improve your knowledge of something already learned but partly forgotten (83)

check up on *pv* to try to discover what someone is doing in order to be certain that they are doing what they should be doing (83)

classification *n* the act or process of dividing things into groups according to their type (80)

come up against *pv* to have to deal with a problem (83)

conscientious *adj* putting a lot of effort into your work (84)

consistently *adv* continuing or developing steadily in the same way (80)

constitute *v* to be or be considered as something (80)

do away with *pv* to get rid of something, or stop using something (83)

extrovert *n* an energetic happy person who enjoys being with other people (80)

get back to *pv* (reply) to talk to someone again, usually on the phone (83)

get through to *pv* to succeed in making someone believe or understand something (83)

idealistic *adj* believing that very good things can be achieved, often when this does not seem likely to others (84)

insecure *adj* Insecure people have little confidence and are uncertain about their own abilities or if other people really like them. (84)

introvert *n* someone who is shy, quiet, and unable to make friends easily (80)

merit *n* the quality of being good and deserving praise (80)

modest *adj* not usually talking about or making obvious your own abilities and achievements (84)

naive *adj* If you are naive, you are too willing to believe that someone is telling the truth, that people's intentions in general are good, or that life is simple and fair. People are often naive because they are young and/or have not had much experience of life. (84)

narrow-minded *adj* not willing to accept ideas or ways of behaving that are different from your own (84)

outgoing *adj* (character) friendly and energetic and finding it easy and enjoyable to be with other people (81)

perception *n* a belief or opinion, often held by many people and based on how things seem (80)

play down *pv* to make something seem less important or less bad than it really is (81)

proposition *n* an idea or opinion (80)

questionable *adj* not certain, or wrong in some way (80)

read up on *pv* to spend time reading in order to find out information about something (83)

self-centred *adj* only interested in yourself and your own activities (84)

self-conscious *adj* nervous or uncomfortable because you are worried what people think about you or your actions (84)

talkative *adj* talking a lot (84)

trustworthy *adj* able to be trusted (84)

ACKNOWLEDGEMENTS

The author and publishers would like to thank Michael Black for writing the Grammar Reference and the Speaking and Writing Guides, and Rawdon Wyatt for writing the CD-ROM.

The author would like to thank Judith Greet, Jane Coates and Una Yeung for their input and efficiency.

The author and publishers would like to thank the following teachers who reviewed the material:

Brazil: Litany Ribeiro; Spain: Catherine Hollins; Switzerland: Lynn Weibel; Russia: Claire Barnes, Irina Basova; UK: Julian Oakley.

Corpus
Development of this publication has made use of the Cambridge English Corpus (CEC). The CEC is a computer database of contemporary spoken and written English, which currently stands at over one billion words. It includes British English, American English and other varieties of English. It also includes the Cambridge Learner Corpus, developed in collaboration with Cambridge English Language Assessment. Cambridge University Press has built up the CEC to provide evidence about language use that helps to produce better language teaching materials.

English Profile
This product is informed by the English Vocabulary Profile, built as part of English Profile, a collaborative programme designed to enhance the learning, teaching and assessment of English worldwide. Its main funding partners are Cambridge University Press and Cambridge English Language Assessment and its aim is to create a 'profile' for English linked to the Common European Framework of Reference for Languages (CEF). English Profile outcomes, such as the English Vocabulary Profile, will provide detailed information about the language that learners can be expected to demonstrate at each CEF level, offering a clear benchmark for learners' proficiency. For more information, please visit www.englishprofile.org

Cambridge Dictionaries
Cambridge dictionaries are the world's most widely used dictionaries for learners of English. The dictionaries are available in print and online at dictionary.cambridge.org. Copyright © Cambridge University Press, reproduced with permission.

Text
The authors and publishers acknowledge the following sources of copyright material and are grateful for the permissions granted. While every effort has been made, it has not always been possible to identify the sources of all the material used, or to trace all copyright holders. If any omissions are brought to our notice, we will be happy to include the appropriate acknowledgements on reprinting.
p. 10, 11 adapted from 'The writing is on the paywall – but the end of print is not quite nigh' (Preston, P) 30/12/2012, The Observer, © Guardian News & Media Ltd 2012; p. 12 adapted from 'The ethics of citizen photography' (Ruokosuo, N) 14/08/2012, The Guardian, © Guardian News & Media Ltd 2012; p. 17 (text A & D) adapted from 'Making a Difference: Volunteer Tourism and Development' (Butcher, J & Smith, P) by permission of Tourism Recreation Research; p. 17 (text B) adapted from 'Impacts of International Volunteering and Service' (Sherraden, MS, Lough, BJ, Moore McBride, A) 2008, Center for Social Development with permission from the authors; p. 17 (text C) adapted from 'International Volunteering for Development and Sustainability: outdated paternalism or a radical response to globalisation?' (Devereux, P) 2008, Development in practice by OXFAM, reproduced with permission of ROUTLEDGE in the format republished in a book/textbook via Copyright Clearance Center. With permission of Taylor & Francis Ltd, http://www.informaworld. com; p. 26, 27 adapted from 'Now everyone is connected, is this the death of conversation?'(Jenkins, S) 26/04/2012, The Guardian, © Guardian News & Media Ltd 2012; p. 32, 33 adapted from 'Make your idea and start selling it: the best way to develop products' (Neves, A) 07/06/2011, The Independent; pp. 48, 49 adapted from 'Online arts: Click-fix culture' (Sturges, F) 06/04/2011, The Independent; p. 58, 59 adapted from 'The end of the road for motormania' (Pearce, F) 16/08/2011, New Scientist, © 2011 Reed Business Information, UK. All rights reserved. Distributed by Tribune Content Agency, LLC; p. 65, adapted from 'Manual of Learning Styles' (Honey, P. & Mumford, A), Learning Styles Questionnaire. © 2006 by Peter Honey, published by Pearson TalentLens, a division of Pearson Education Ltd; p. 74, 75 adapted from 'Science on TV: it's not dumb, but it could be smarter' (Bell, A) 17/02/2013, The Observer, © Guardian News & Media Ltd 2013; p. 76 adapted from 'Hold the line: Overheard phone calls more distracting than room full of people chatting' (Connor, S) 13/03/2013, The Independent; p. 80 adapted from 'Quiz: are you an introvert?' 13/03/2012, © Guardian News & Media Ltd 2012; p. 81 (Text B) adapted from 'Quiet: the Power of Introverts in a World That Can't Stop Talking by Susan Cain: review' (Payne,T) 23/03/2012, Daily Telegraph, © Telegraph Media Group Limited 2012; p. 81 (Text C) adapted from 'Quiet: The Power of Introverts in a World That Can't Stop Talking' by Susan Cain – review' (Sawyer, M & Maitland, S) 18/03/2012, The Observer, © Guardian News & Media Ltd 2012.

Photos
Thanks to the following for permission to reproduce copyright photographs:

L = Left, CL = Centre left, CR = Centre right, R = Right

p. 8(A) Shutterstock.com/Paul Fleet; p. 8(B) Shutterstock.com/ ShNarongsak Nagadhana; p. 8(C) Shutterstock.com/Catmando; p. 8(D) Shutterstock.com/Paulo M. F. Pires; p.10 (online Observer) Alamy/ Clynt Garnham Technology; p. 10 (online Magazine) Alamy/NetPhotos; p. 10 (Kindle) Alamy/Martin Williams; p. 13 Alamy/MBI; p. 14 (luxury car) Alamy/niceartphoto; p. 14 (soup kitchen) Alamy/EPA European Pressphoto Agency b.v.; p. 16 (volunteer at Huruma school) Alamy/ Sean Sprague; p. 16 (volunteers building homes) Alamy/David Cole; p. 16 (volunteer at a primary School) Corbis/Hugh Sitton; p. 20 (Inti Raymi festival) Alamy/Keren Su/China Span; p. 20 (llama figure) Alamy/ imagebroker; p. 21(1) Alamy/PhotosIndia.com LLC; p. 21(2) SuperStock/ Blend Images; p. 21(3) Alamy/Blend Images; p. 22(1) Alamy/Carl Howe LLC; p. 22(2) Alamy/M. Scott Brauer; p. 22(3) Alamy/Cath Evans; p. 23 Alamy/Pat Behnke; p. 24 (family) Shutterstock.com/Monkey Business Images; p. 24 (mother and child) Shutterstock.com/Wavebreakmedia; p. 24 (students) Shutterstock.com/Mike Flippo; p. 24 (couple) Shutterstock.com/Spotmatik; p. 26 (business people) Alamy/MBI; p. 26 (train) SuperStock/BE&W; p. 26 (family dinner) Corbis/Image Source; p. 29 Shutterstock.com/Vasiliy Ganzha; p. 32 Phil Pinnell, Scratch Meals; p. 37 Shutterstock.com/ESTUDI M6; p. 38 Images Courtesy of The Advertising Archives; p. 40 (GP) Shutterstock.com/Alexander Raths; p. 40 (surgeon) Alamy/Universal Images Group Limited; p. 40 (paramedics) Alamy/CandyBox Images; p. 42(1) Shutterstock.com/Peter Kirillov; p. 42(2) Shutterstock.com/W Mimohe; p. 42(3) Shutterstock. com/Olga Besnard; p. 42(4) Shutterstock.com/Jeff Lim C.W; p.42(5) Shutterstock.com/Muzsy; p. 44 Alamy/Velosport; p. 45(1) Alamy/PCN Photography; p. 45(2) Corbis/ANDREW WINNING/Reuters; p. 45(3) Getty Images; p. 46 AFP/Getty Images; p. 48 (traditional painting) Alamy/David Coleman; p. 48 (modern art) Alamy/Gay Tourism; p. 48 (Marriage of Figaro) Alamy/age fotostock; p. 48 (Black Eyed Peas) Alamy/RIA Novosti; p. 48 (La Tempestad) Getty Images; p. 52 (football collection) Alamy/Oso Media; p. 52 (photography) Alamy/Eddie Gerald; p. 52 (posters) Alamy/Randy Duchaine; p. 53 Shutterstock. com/Kushch Dmitry; p. 54 (Goldfinger) Alamy/AF Archive; p. 54 (Skyfall) REX/Snap Stills; p. 56 (rainforest) Shutterstock.com/Sittitap; p. 56 (Bernese Alps) Shutterstock.com/Pecold; p. 56 (trees and river) Shutterstock.com/Kevin Eaves; p. 58 (light traffic) Shutterstock.com/ Tupungato; p. 58 (traffic jam) Shutterstock.com/Tupungato; p. 58 (gridlock) Shutterstock.com/Chungking; p. 62(A) Shutterstock.com/ Jeannette Katzir Photog; p. 62(B) Shutterstock.com/Harald Toepfer; p. 62(C) Shutterstock.com/John Michael Evan Potter; p. 62(D) Alamy/ Blickwinkel; p. 64(L) Alamy/AberCPC; p. 64(CL) Alamy/Photolibrary; p. 64(CR) Shutterstock.com/Robert Kneschke; p. 64(R) Alamy/Blend Images; p. 68 Alamy/Horizons WWP; p. 70 (carer) Alamy/Angela Hampton; p. 70 (waiter) Alamy/Peter Titmuss; p. 72 (science lesson) Alamy/Age Fotostock; p. 72 (science experiment) Alamy/Image Source; p. 74 (mad scientist) Shutterstock.com/Jeanne McRight; p. 74 (medical researcher) Alamy/Hongqi Zhang; p. 77(1) Shutterstock.com/Goodluz; p. 77(2) Alamy/Age Fotostock; p. 77(3) Shutterstock.com/Goodluz; p. 78 (astronomers) SuperStock/Visions of America; p. 78 (space) NASA; p. 80 (reading) Alamy/Image Source Plus; p. 80 (dancing) Alamy/Blend Images; p. 84 Alamy/Cultura RM.

Illustrations
John Batten p. 18; Nick Duffy pp. 25, 36, 50, 57, 66, 73; Mark Duffin p. 30; Richard Jones pp. 35, 82

Recordings by Leon Chambers at The Soundhouse Ltd.

Picture research by Sarah Deakin.

System Requirements

Windows
- Intel® Pentium® 4 2GHz or faster
- Microsoft Windows® XP (SP3), Vista® (SP2), Windows® 7, Windows 8
- Minimum 750MB of hard drive space
- Adobe® Flash® Player 10.3.183.7 or later

Mac
- Intel® Core™ Duo 1.83GHz or faster
- Mac OS X® 10.5 or later
- Minimum 1GB RAM
- Minimum 750 of hard drive space
- Adobe® Flash® Player 10.3.183.7 or later

Installation Instructions

Insert the Compact Advanced CD-ROM into your CD-DVD drive. Follow the installation instructions on your screen.

Windows

On a Windows PC, if the CD-ROM does not automatically start, open My Computer, locate your CD-DVD drive and open it to view the content of the CD-ROM. double-click on the CambridgeApplicationInstaller file. Follow the installation instructions on your screen.

Mac

On a Mac, if the CD-ROM does not automatically start to install, double-click on the CompactAdvanced CD icon on your desktop. Double-click on the CambridgeApplicationInstaller file. Follow the instructions on your screen.

Technical support

For support visit our website: www.cambridge.org/elt/multimedia/help